The Ref's Call

Owen Doyle is a former international rugby union referee, who retired in 1994. He was Director of Referees at the Irish Rugby Football Union (IRFU) from 1995 to 2015 and an elite referee coach from 2015 to 2017. Now a rugby columnist with *The Irish Times*, Owen Doyle lives in Dublin.

The Ref's Call

Memoir of a Rugby Referee

Owen Doyle

HACHETTE
BOOKS
IRELAND

First published in Ireland in 2022 by
HACHETTE BOOKS IRELAND

1

Cataloguing in Publication Data is available from the British Library

ISBN 9781529396058

Typeset in Eames Century Mode by
Palimpsest Book Production Ltd, Falkirk, Stirlingshire

Printed and bound in Great Britain by
Clays Ltd, Elcograf, S.p.A

Hachette Books Ireland policy is to use papers that are natural, renewable
and recyclable products and made from wood grown in sustainable forests.
The logging and manufacturing processes are expected to conform
to the environmental regulations of the country of origin.

Hachette Books Ireland
8 Castlecourt Centre
Castleknock
Dublin 15, Ireland

A division of Hachette UK Ltd
Carmelite House, 50 Victoria Embankment, EC4Y 0DZ

www.hachettebooksireland.ie

For Mark and Ian,
&
for Beth and Jamie

Foreword

'Who'd be a referee?'

How many times have I stood on the terraces of club grounds all over the country or sat in the stand or press box at the highest level of the game and wondered why, with so much abuse being hurled at the person wielding the whistle in the centre of the action, would you bother.

Thankfully, there's a magnificent cohort of men and women who enable our great game to function every weekend by putting their hands up and taking responsibility for keeping law and order in one of the most complex sports to adjudicate on.

Even after fifty years of active involvement in rugby, be it on the field of play or sitting in the press or commentary box, I still come across situations that cause confusion, with the continual tweaking of the laws and the varying interpretation of those laws from one hemisphere to the other.

I write the foreword to this excellent insight on the game – produced courtesy of not only a great Irish referee but an outstanding administrator who made a profound impact on rugby on the global stage – having just returned from Ireland's historic series-winning tour of New Zealand in the summer of 2022.

Never has top-level rugby been more difficult or challenging for our referees, as evidenced by an alarming series of blunders made, on and off the field, in Ireland's historic first ever win over the All Blacks on opposition soil, in Dunedin in a chaotic second test.

At one stage New Zealand should have been reduced to 12 players due to a sequence of incidents that led to a yellow and a red card being issued to both New Zealand tight-head props in the space of a few minutes, eventually leading to a period of uncontested scrums.

New Zealand's most influential forward, Ardie Savea, temporally withdrawn to facilitate the introduction of a front row replacement, should have been allowed back on the field on the completion of the yellow card and the recommencement of contested scrums, but was refused by the fourth official.

Chaos ensued, with nobody really sure what was happening. No wonder one highly respected referee I met on my journey home felt completely exposed and let down by those in charge at the very highest levels.

When the game turned professional in 1995, having just called time on an outstanding career as a top-class international referee, Owen Doyle stepped forward and took on the newly created role of director of referees with the IRFU.

With a blank canvas and a minute budget, Doyle led the way in devising a world-class programme designed to not only produce officials for the domestic game in Ireland but referees capable of reaching the pinnacle of their profession and establishing themselves at the very top of the international game.

In his 20 years at the helm of Irish rugby's refereeing department, the IRFU's model became best in class, with outstanding officials such as Alan Lewis, Donal Courtney, Helen O'Reilly, Joy Neville, George Clancy and Johnny Lacey all making their mark on the international stage.

Perhaps Owen's greatest success was in persuading former Irish international scrum half Alain Rolland to make the transition from international player to referee. When Rolland was given the ultimate honour of refereeing the 2007 World Cup final at the Stade de France in Paris between South Africa and England, Doyle was entitled to sit back and reflect on a job well done.

As a referee, Owen Doyle carried huge respect during my time as a player, up there with the very best in a long line of quality Irish international officials. Owen had presence on the field, something hugely important for the man with the whistle. Sometimes, just a look from him was sufficient to remind you who was in charge.

He wasn't short of a word either in the midst of battle. I remember one of my early games as a budding second row, playing for UCC against Blackrock in Stradbrook when, after a lineout, Doyle addressed me as I ran across the field. 'Let the real jumpers jump,' he said.

I was marking someone that day who was openly being tipped for Leinster and possibly Irish honours in the future. I was also beginning to attract the interest of the Munster selectors at the time and, as someone who prided myself on my athletic ability, was taken aback by Doyle's comment.

It registered, and spurred me into action. As I proceeded to dominate my highly fancied opponent, I could see the smile on Doyle's face as the game progressed. To this day, I'm not sure whether he was goading me or if he was serious.

The Ref's Call

About a decade later, when Munster drew with Ulster in Ravenhill in 1989, I was awarded a dubious try, under a pile of bodies, having taken a peel off the tail of the lineout. As I trotted back for the restart, Owen enquired, 'You did get the ball down, didn't you?'

'Of course I did, Owen.'

Had a television match official been in place in Belfast that day, he might not have agreed.

That's the challenge for the modern-day referee. With so much input from his two assistants, the TMOs and fourth official, their authority and decision-making is constantly under review. It has become an increasingly difficult job. That's where common sense comes into play, and where people with the experience of Owen Doyle are sadly missed.

For me, the ground rules changed the day referees were 'miked up' for all to hear live on television. That addition has been brilliant in keeping the audience informed and up to speed with the reasons behind the various decisions but, in addition, the cult of the referee becoming a personality in their own right was created. The genie was out of the bottle. Let's just say some could handle it better than others. The old adage that the best referees are the ones that go unnoticed over the course of the 80 minutes was thrown out the window straight away.

Owen Doyle

Arguably, Owen's biggest contribution to rugby came during his time as director of referees with the IRFU, where he displayed an incredible ability to get things done. He brought organisation and professionalism to a newly established position, and oversaw a mentoring and coaching programme that saw the IRFU produce more international-standard rugby officials than any other country at that time.

Perhaps Doyle's greatest achievement was his input into – and influence over – the proposed introduction of a series of law changes following a number of trial games conducted at Stellenbosch University in South Africa in 2006.

Backed by the International Rugby Board, these trials resulted in the creation of 24 experimental law variations – ELVs as they became known – to be road-tested in both hemispheres before being adopted into law.

Designed to make the game more free-flowing, and with huge support from Australia, whose own rugby union faced massive competition for bums on seats from a number of other professional sports, including rugby league, Australian Rules, soccer and cricket, some of the proposed changes would, in effect, get rid of the maul and de-power the scrum, and in doing so change the very fundamentals of the game.

Doyle led the charge in designing a reasoned and well-constructed case as to why several of these proposals would damage the game. With the strong backing of the RFU in England, the arguments put forward resulted in the major game-changing initiatives being rejected.

This excellent memoir reveals the background to some of those key decisions, it takes us behind the scenes of some of the most memorable games and tournaments, and offers a rare insight into how the role of the modern-day referee has evolved and is managed in the professional era.

The Ref's Call is a compelling read and a valuable historical record on the development of rugby, both domestically and internationally, that will prove a valuable resource and reference point for journalists and supporters alike.

His vast experience and knowledge resonates through each and every chapter and, in doing so, Owen continues to serve the game that has shaped and influenced his life since his early days in schools rugby.

Donal Lenihan, August 2022

Chapter One

21 January 1984

*Wales v Scotland, National Stadium, Cardiff Arms Park
(Opening day of that year's Five Nations)*

*Suddenly, we were on our way. Nothing can prepare you for the
roar that greeted the teams as they ran out into the great stadium
that is Cardiff Arms Park. It was exhilarating and the anthems
only added to the wonderful atmosphere. First, 'Flower of
Scotland' and then the emotional rendition of 'Mae Hen Wlad
Fy Nhadau', ('Land of My Fathers'), passionately sung by a
Welsh choir of thousands. There is no place on Earth quite like it.*

*I did not hear my own whistle as I got things started, the
noise was so deafening, rolling out of the stands in thunderous
waves, with Welsh hymns reverberating around the stadium. I
remember shaking the whistle up against my ear to make sure*

1

the 'pea' was still there and that it was actually working. It was disorientating, even surreal, bringing the realisation that this was going to be one very new experience, despite everything I had done up until that moment.

As a young boy, sitting rapt with my father and brother in front of our black-and-white TV, I had always watched this moment in Cardiff, in total awe every year – and now here I was, slap bang in the middle of it, an international Test match. Perhaps my own part in the scene wasn't exactly how I'd pictured it in my boyhood dreams, but it was, nonetheless, extraordinary.

• • •

It was the perfect drop kick. Textbook. Not until Jonny Wilkinson, Ronan O'Gara and Johnny Sexton came along to produce their own magic would that kick be equalled. The mighty Monsieur 'Le Drop' of that era – France's Pierre Albaladejo – would have thoroughly approved.

My 10-year-old self watched in wonder as the ball sailed through the makeshift bamboo goalposts,, imagining my kick was the one that would ensure an Ireland victory over England that day. Very quickly, though, my fascination turned to horror. The ball was still rising when it smashed through the single-glazed window of my father's small home office. I dropped to my knees, waiting for the parental wrath which would surely follow.

But my father didn't appear for some time. When he did, it was to look out at me through the window frame and calmly beckon to join him. I quickly obeyed, quaking inwardly. But while his desk and chair, which faced the window, were covered in splintered glass, with shards embedded in the chair and in the blotter pad, there he stood, unscathed and unbloodied. It seemed he had left the office just moments before to make a cup of tea, which was a huge relief and a luckier break than I usually got.

He knew that I understood just how lucky we both were, and that there was no need for harsh words. There was no anger or recrimination from him – instead, just a very unexpected question: 'What foot did you kick that with?' It had been my left, and that was the first time I realised that I could kick equally well with both feet, a skill which would later prove very useful on the pitch. It's also probably the quid pro quo reason why I have two left hands when it comes to DIY.

Looking back now, I see that this incident was important in that it perfectly encapsulated a key part of my father's philosophy in life, which he passed on to me and my siblings – that it was fine to make mistakes, as long as you used them as opportunities to learn or discover something new.

Every afternoon, hail, rain – which it was mostly – or even shine, Ireland would play an international rugby match in the back garden of that happy home in Dartry.

I contrived, all at once, to be the thirty players, the referee, and even the commentator, who was always the BBC's Bill

McLaren, 'the voice of rugby'. Even then, I was certain that one day I'd pull on an Irish jersey, which I expected would have had the number 15 on its back. What I couldn't have known was that 25 years later, McLaren would commentate on international matches in which I'd be wearing the green of Ireland, albeit a referee's jersey.

My father, Eddie Doyle, was steeped in sports and a gifted athlete himself, though we had to find that out for ourselves over the years – he never spoke of, let alone boasted about, his own achievements.

He had played on the first two Belvedere College rugby teams to win the Leinster Schools Senior Cup in 1923 and 1924. After he left school, an All-Ireland Youth athletics gold medal was added to his accolades. Not to mention more long-distance swimming medals than you can imagine, including one for winning the 1931 Liffey swim – an annual event immortalised in the famous Jack Yeats painting showing the hordes of Dubliners who would line the banks of the river to cheer on those taking part. In fact, he had nearly won the race when he was only 12 years old, but, with quite a handsome lead, he sadly sank under O'Connell Bridge and had to be pulled out. Again, it was one of his friends who told me that, rather than him.

After playing for many years for Clontarf FC, Eddie took up some refereeing of his own, making it to interprovincial level before ultimately becoming president of the Association of Referees, Leinster Branch; and then finished his career in sports administration as president of the Branch.

In his mid-60s, he decided that he'd take up sailing, a sport in which my brother Ross excelled. Of course, simply pottering around Dublin bay wasn't enough for him – he had to join a club so he could sail competitively. The average age of the beginners' class in Dún Laoghaire is normally around 14, so that figure must have really been skewed the year Eddie joined. Typically, he insisted on throwing an end-of-term party for his classmates; fortunately, my mother was there to remind him that beer should not be served.

There was little that seemed beyond him, and after he passed away in 2007 (aged 90), we found photographs of him halfway up the Matterhorn and canoeing the Rhine – taken at a time when most Dubliners were wondering how to get to London. This summed up another important part of my father's take on life – that it was okay to branch out and try new things, as long as you did it for the sheer joy of taking part and gave it your all.

My mother, Béatrice Pélissier – known as 'Betty' by family and friends – was also a colourful character with a very interesting background. Her father Edward Pélissier's family had fled France during the infamous persecution of the Huguenots; her mother, Helen Mooney, was Irish. Tragically, my grandfather had been killed in a freak accident when my mother was still very young. He had just dropped the family off at a hotel near Blessington in County Wicklow, and was in the process of turning his car when it stalled on the railway tracks; it was too late for the driver of an approaching train to avoid the inevitable, fatal collision.

In time, my grandmother got married again – to Frank Collins, who worked in India with the British government. This meant that my mother had an unusual childhood with plenty of foreign travel. As well as making the return journey to India several times with her mother to see her stepfather – travelling from Dublin to Durban by boat and rail and then on to India by another sea voyage – she lived and was educated in exotic places that were continents away, including Karachi and Cape Town, with Wesley College her Irish alma mater. In all, the family moved house 18 times.

Betty was an upbeat, happy person who was never in bad form. She always encouraged our childhood enthusiasms – mine for rugby, Ross's for sailing, my sisters Adrienne and Linda inherited her love for hockey – and didn't seem to mind that our back garden had the appearance of an oft-used mudbath, while the neighbours' lawns, rose bushes and shrubbery were manicured and immaculately laid out. It was all in the interests of my rugby career – like my father, she believed you should seize the day and give things your best shot.

As well as being a tolerant, fun-loving mother to us, Betty was very beautiful. It wasn't a surprise for us to find out as children that she had once passed an initial screen test with MGM – though she had turned the follow-up down flat. I remember being quite miffed when I learned this – I felt my own Hollywood aspirations had never had the chance to get off the ground, because Betty had scuppered any helpful connections she could have made there.

The Ref's Call

'Why on earth did you turn it down?' I asked indignantly.

'Oh, that's easy,' she replied at once, 'it was because I'd met your dad.'

I never could accept that as a valid excuse – not until much later in my life anyway.

By the time I was in my teens, my father's active days in sport were behind him. But he was still very much involved in the world of rugby, and had taken on some new, really interesting roles within the game. One of these was acting as liaison officer for incoming touring sides during the 1950s and '60s – Avril Malan's Springboks, Wilson Whineray's All Blacks and John Thornett's Wallabies.

It encompassed the time that the Wallabies had serious trouble in their second match of the 1966 tour, against Oxford University at Iffley Road, when their hooker Ross Cullen notoriously sank his teeth into the earlobe of Irishman Ollie Waldron. The condition of Waldron's ear confirmed the worst and Cullen was despatched on the next available Sydney-bound flight, never to pull on his country's jersey again.

The same year, Ireland recorded a famous victory against that Australian team, winning 15–8. In that match too, there was trouble, and Irish debutant Noel 'Noisy' Murphy was poleaxed by a very efficient Wallaby punch from Nick Shehadie who was later knighted and became mayor of Sydney. Neither accolade, I understand, was for the punch.

Murphy ended his career the way it had started when, in his final match in 1969, he was felled with one of the most infamous punches in Five Nations history. This time the perpetrator was Brian Price of Wales, who claimed that he had been provoked. The Scottish referee, Dougie McMahon, only awarded a penalty.

It all meant that my parents played host to a number of really fascinating and famous elite rugby men who came to our home for lunch or afternoon tea. The stories they told and the fun they were having persuaded me that, as well as playing for Ireland, I'd have to go on a Lions tour as well.

One of these visitors was a well-known Frenchman and, as my mother told us days in advance of his arrival, the owner of an extraordinarily large nose. She warned us again and again, almost continuously in fact, that when we met this man, we were on no account to stare or giggle at the nose, but instead to simply say 'Hello', shake his hand and leave the room immediately. When the big day finally came, we were ushered in to meet the man in question (his nose really was huge), and my mother announced, 'Now, children, I'd like you to meet . . . Mr Nose.'

Fortunately, after a few moments of stunned silence, the house shook with laughter, and even Mr Nose joined in the fun. It was proof, if any was needed, that Betty's charm could get her through the trickiest of situations! A few days later, I was happy to accept an increase in pocket money, in exchange for a promise to stop mimicking the famous introduction.

My father's other rugby role was to look after all the

referees who came to Dublin for Ireland's home matches. They too came to our house and I learned that, contrary to popular opinion, these men were perfectly normal human beings.

One of the first to visit us was Welshman Gwynne Walters, very small of stature, but huge of heart. Always quietly spoken, his Welsh lilt was never raised, even when refereeing. He would insist on dancing with my mother; since she was about the same height as him, he said, this meant that he could look into her eyes as they waltzed around the living room to the music of Richard Strauss, scratching out from the old record player.

I'll never forget one year he came to referee an Ireland v France match, which I was able to go and see. I was seated on the old touchline seats that existed then and, while the view wasn't great, when play was nearby, you were almost part of the action yourself. The next day, Sunday, before returning home, Walters turned up unexpectedly at Dartry Road and handed me a French jersey. Then he was gone before a speechless boy could thank him.

Another intriguing visitor in those days was English referee Air Vice-Marshal 'Larry' Lamb. Lamb had had a long career in the RAF, including the final years of the Second World War, and was much admired for it. He was a very interesting character and, as his position demanded, was not lacking one iota of self-assurance. The stories of his flying days and of his post-war involvement in the Berlin

Airlift never failed to fascinate me. He refereed several internationals at Lansdowne Road, once notably being unsighted for a glaring knock-on by Irish wing Eddie Grant, who went on to score. In those days, with no assistance on the sidelines or from a television match official (TMO), one split second of inattention could lead to an error of that kind. I doubt, though, if anyone had the nerve to bring it up with the air vice-marshal after the match. It was all part of rugby in those days.

In his 'day job', my father was a wine agent, as was his father before him. As such, he didn't handle the goods, but instructed various producers to ship directly to his clients in Ireland, such as the Shelbourne Hotel. It's amazing to think that in that era the hotel bought their generic Bordeaux wines in bulk, subsequently having them bottled by Mitchell & Son, who, to this day, are still a family concern, currently being run by its seventh generation.

As part of his work, Eddie would frequently travel to France to check out the quality of the wines, and his connections there were widespread, something I was to benefit from, both as a teenager and in later life. Every so often, my mother would go with him and these were trips they both loved. They'd also go to London together at least once a year, and, while it was business, it's clear that the candlelit dinners and West End shows were the really enjoyable part of the experience.

Since both of my parents were widely travelled

– particularly Betty, given her roving childhood – they were keen for me to experience other countries and cultures from an early age. Given my mother's heritage and my father's strong networks of business contacts who had become friends, France seemed like a good place to start. And so neither of them gave a second thought to putting me, alone, on a plane to Paris at the age of 12, suitably identified by a plastic-encased card hung around my neck – in case I got lost, I suppose. How those innocent times have changed; parents would probably be arrested for attempting the same thing today.

In Paris, I was met by Béatrice Lawton, the daughter of my father's good friend Jean, and all of 15 years old at the time. Together, we took the overnight train to Bordeaux's Gare St Jean, where the immense figure of her father was standing on the platform, waiting to meet us. Over the years, Jean would meet me many times on that platform. He became a sort of assistant-father to me, for which I felt very fortunate.

On that first trip, we immediately drove to the Lawtons' summer house among the pines in Cap Ferret, with the Atlantic on one side of the peninsula and the Bassin d'Arcachon on the other. I spent a full month there, barely speaking – not a word of French would come out of my mouth. But I loved it. When I went back the following summer, it was a very pleasant surprise to realise that I quickly understood every word. Soon the words started to come too, and I was able to chat away in French.

Giving me the opportunity to learn a different language was another way my parents helped to set me up for the future – not only with my work in the wine trade when I decided to take over my father's business, but in my role as an international referee. I was one of the few who was able to decipher what the players on the French XV were saying to each other during play, and who could converse with the captain and coach before or after a match. So much so that former England captain Will Carling would politely ask that I translate into English every word I uttered in French!

Jean Lawton had five daughters, no less, and after a few years of my annual visits, he and his wife Evelyn decided that I might be better off in the company of some boys of my own age. So they introduced me to a fellow wine merchant, Yves Hanappier, who had three sons, and I soon found myself on the other side of the Bassin d'Arcachon, in Le Moulleau.

Wonderful times followed, learning to sail in very warm climes and living in swimming shorts. When I was about 16, the singer Françoise Hardy came to town. I was instantly smitten when she smiled at me as we both stood in a queue to buy ice-creams – but just as quickly devastated when she hopped into a waiting vehicle that looked very much like a Ferrari, driven by someone who was also out of my league, which all seemed very unfair.

In those long school holidays, when I'd returned from my usual month-long sojourn in France, I'd rush to join the family who would spend the summer weeks on the beaches and in the seas of Ardamine and Poulshone in Wexford, where my parents rented a holiday home. It was actually more of a shack than a house, wonderfully primitive and situated in a hollow beside the beach.

We boated, swam, fished and kayaked, no matter the waves or the weather. It's a mystery how we all survived. The kayaks were uncomfortable, so we'd sit on our lifejackets; and we were supplied with a tube of Bostik glue, a few old ice-pop sticks for spreading the stuff and some squares of canvas. Whenever necessary, and that was often, we'd have to head swiftly for land or kayak-surf into Courtown Harbour to carry out much-needed running repairs.

I remember clearly how, when he was about 11, Ross fixed a makeshift sail to one of the kayaks, and promptly shot across the bay and past Roney Rock. My father luckily managed to intercept him just before he disappeared from view, with the Azores probably being the next stopping point. The young sailor, always much braver than I was, was very disappointed to be towed home.

There's a lot of coastal erosion along that Wexford coast-line, and a long time after we had grown up and no longer holidayed there, the house at Ardamine was taken away by the winter storms and high tides. When I heard, I drove down to see what, if anything, remained. I walked along the beach, the sea was rolling, and I looked southwards towards Roney Point, with its landmark rock some way offshore – that was that was our maximum 'travel allowance' on the waves but, of course, we'd venture further south whenever the mood took us. I found myself thinking that we must have been totally mad at the time, or perhaps it was just our youthful belief that we were somehow invincible.

When I got to the place where we had spent so many happy hours, all that remained was the corner of the old kitchen stove sticking up from the sand. But while the house was gone, I could still see it in my mind's eye, just sitting there as always: that spot will forever hold magical memories for me. So much so that, for years after those happy family holidays and to this day, the house at Ardamine and the nearby beach are the places I've revisited in my thoughts when life has been at its most challenging.

Later in my career, I took on elite referee coaching and I always emphasised the key value of learning from a poor performance or making rookie mistakes – that's what the purpose of any post-match analysis should be, rather than dwelling too long on negative and pointless self-criticism. In my own time officiating, I'd found it important to start the analysis of a poor performance by 'walking the beach', sometimes figuratively, sometimes in reality. I found that being alone, in the company of the sun and the sea, provided a place of true calmness that enabled me to put everything into perspective, and, to paraphrase the words immortalised in song by Frank Sinatra, to get back up, dust myself off and start over. If there wasn't a beach nearby, I'd close my eyes and imagine I was back in Ardamine.

Chapter Two

18 December 1977

Ulster v Munster in Ravenhill
(Final day of that year's interprovincial championships)

Munster hacked the ball through and, as it bobbled along the ground, Ulster's wonderful centre Mike Gibson was deciding whether to pick it up or drop down on it. At that very moment, Munster's Colm Tucker came through to foot-rush the ball further downfield.

Suddenly, the ball was now fair game for Tucker, who caught both it and Gibson – who had bravely dived towards the ground – with his boot. I viewed it as an accident; otherwise, it had to be a sending-off offence. As it still the case today, there is sometimes very little between those two extremes – accidental or a red card.

Despite Gibson being a boyhood hero of mine and his shoulder injury forcing him out of the game, I could not let that affect my decision-making.

Needless to say, Ulster were livid, with not even a penalty kick awarded. All explanations that I felt it was not Tucker's fault fell on deaf ears.

• • •

During the 1964 Five Nations, Ireland went to Twickenham to take on England, in what would be an epic, history-making encounter. I'd not long turned 15 and still remember clearly the sense of excitement and anticipation we felt as our family sat around our black-and-white TV to watch the match on that early February afternoon. We were all keen to see how our new out-half would play – at the time, nobody outside Ulster had heard much about Mike Gibson, other than that the Ireland selectors had been mightily impressed with his performance for Cambridge against Oxford the previous December.

For the next 80 minutes, we watched, mesmerised, as Gibson carved England apart. Ireland scored four tries and he created most – if not all – of them. Every rugby fan has their favourite tries, of course. While it's well-nigh impossible to pick the best of all time, Ireland's famous criss-cross try at that Five Nations match, initiated by Gibson, is right up there with the very best, as far as I'm concerned. But he couldn't have done it without his two partners in crime that day, Jerry Walsh from Cork and Pat Casey of UCD and Lansdowne.

As Gibson cut through the middle, he reverse-passed to Walsh who was heading to the right. Casey decided he liked the look of what was happening and, steaming in from his right-wing position, took another reverse pass from Walsh. Then, at full pelt, Casey stormed past the rest of the bedraggled defence and scored underneath the posts. If any English player had managed to get a hand to him, it was a despairing one. It was spontaneously thrilling and inspiring to me; we knew we were watching history being made.

Thanks to the wonders of the internet, that moment can be relived time and again today. The final score was 18–5 to Ireland, 26–7 in today's money, so it was quite a thrashing for England. If anybody had told me then that one day I'd be on the same pitch as Mike Gibson, I'd have had them straitjacketed and led away.

In the meantime, my own schoolboy rugby career had started in earnest, and I was enjoying it even more than those back-garden games. After primary school, I had been enrolled in St Conleth's College, a smallish school on Dublin's leafy Clyde Road which, happily, continues to thrive there to this day.

It was a great environment for academic learning and had a fine array of teaching staff, prince among them Michael Gardiner, who was in charge of English. He told the class not to be afraid of essay writing: 'Just tell me a story, in your own words' simplified the whole idea. I can still hear his voice today, and I'm still listening.

At the other end of the spectrum was the French teacher, a Breton nationalist, Louis Feutren, whose methods were far removed from the gentlemanly Gardiner. Feutren, never slow to punish, administered quite a thrashing to a young John Terry. Thankfully, Terry survived, otherwise we would never have heard of the great rock band Hurricane Johnny and the Jets; and Trinity College, the oldest continuous rugby club in existence, would not have had Terry as a two-term president.

Feutren told us that he had come to Ireland to flee the invading Germans during the Second World War. Later on, we learned that the truth was very much the reverse: he was a Nazi sympathiser and was actually running from the French resistance. I don't think anybody was overly surprised at the new, correct version of events.

Another Conleth classmate Ken Byrne would, much later on, become my solicitor. It was a rich irony that he, with no interest whatsoever in the oval ball, should carry out his training under the auspices of the Halley firm in Waterford. In contrast to Byrne, Gerry Halley, a true rugby nut, was a very useful player, packing down for University College Dublin at number eight, flanked by Irish internationals Fergus Slattery and Shay Deering.

Unfortunately, when it came to rugby at Conleth, although we strove with might and main, we didn't win many matches. Kevin Kelleher, the headmaster, was reluctant to enter the team in the Leinster Schools cups, for fear of heavy defeats. Kelleher was, of course, one of the outstanding international rugby referees of his generation, and had gained considerable notoriety in 1963 for his sending off of New Zealand's iconic second row Colin 'Pinetree' Meads, when the All Blacks played Scotland that year. Years later travelled Kelleher would travel to New Zealand as the surprise guest for Mead's *This Is Your Life* television show, presenting the great forward with the whistle he had blown at that fateful moment all those years before.

The school did enter the Leinster Senior and Junior Schools cups one year; however, not only did we make little headway in either competition, we sustained several bad injuries. John Bouchier-Hayes, who would go on to represent Ireland in fencing at three Olympic Games, suffered an agonising break to his femur; his kneecap seemed to end up halfway down his shin. There was another painful broken limb the same day and, as very bad luck would have it, the injured party was his brother, Michael. John was left with quite a limp, and it was only thanks to amazing, Herculean effort that he was able to continue his fencing career so successfully.

With the school situated in Ballsbridge, Conleth's home ground was Wanderers FC on the Merrion Road. While this was a good location, it was a dreadful trek back to our house in Dartry, requiring me to take two buses. The first of these was the seemingly very rare number 18, which had its terminus opposite the British embassy. Long waits in the rain were quite the norm before a bus would finally turn up to take me as far as Rathmines. There, I'd hop off and have another wait for a number 14 to get me home.

My father would sometimes come and collect me – and when he did, it was a huge relief. On one occasion, he arrived before the match was over. I was delighted that he was there to see me score a try – at least until the referee disallowed it, a terrible decision in my pre-teenage view. I screamed at him in frustration, and got penalised for my trouble. Afterwards, as I threw my school and kit bags into the car in a strop, my father immediately grabbed them and threw them out again.

'Never do that again, Owen,' he said, in clipped tones. 'You can take the bus today.' Hours later, a drowned rat arrived home. A lesson learned.

With the final played at Lansdowne Road and large crowds watching throughout, being involved at the business end of the Senior Cup was essential for any aspiring young rugby player. It became clear that if I wanted that involvement, I'd have to change school to one of the traditional powerhouses – which, being really happy in Conleth's, I was reluctant to do. After much discussion, however, I moved to my father's alma mater, Belvedere College, on Great Denmark Street, north of Dublin's River Liffey. As the crow flies, it was the school the furthest distance from our home in Dartry. And since buses can't take as direct a route as a crow, it was a long, long way for me to travel there and back each day.

Very shortly after my arrival in Belvedere, the Junior Cup team was picked for the first match of the season. The team sheet was pinned up by the JCT coach, Gerry Spillane SJ, and my name was on the list. While I had played a few matches for Conleth's against Belvedere, no one really knew who I was, other than that I was a blow-in who had mysteriously been selected, leapfrogging others onto the team in the process. The captain, Michael Loughnane, was less than amused at this turn of events and sought me out in the schoolyard. When he found me, he simply said, 'You better be bloody good, Doyle.'

Luckily, my name stayed on that sheet for most of my time in Belvedere, and we made it to two semi-finals, but no further. We were unlucky not to beat a very, very good St Mary's College team that had the great international wing-forward-to-be Shay Deering, along with Peter Boylan, another terrific back-rower and as hard a tackler as you could come across. Somewhat incongruously, Boylan would go on to become the master of the National Maternity Hospital in Holles Street, bringing hundreds of babies into the world and making a wonderful contribution to women's health. Despite the many bone-shaking tackles I endured from him, we have remained in touch.

St Mary's also had Greg Smyth as their fleet-footed star in the centre and Henry Russell-Murphy, a very fine out-half. He benefited, of course, from the slick service of scrum-half Johnny Moloney, later of Ireland and British and Irish Lions fame. Moloney was ridiculously quick and was the schoolboy 440 metres champion. I recall all too well, going in to tackle him as he sped down the touchline at Donnybrook – he was in my sights, there was no way I could miss him. But his long, completely deceptive stride changed gear and, as I dived towards where he had been a split second before, I found only an empty space. Meanwhile, he was running in under our posts and dotting down for a vital try. All through my school career that Mary's team was one to be feared.

The other team to be avoided was Blackrock – who, to this day, are the front-runners of schools rugby, and Senior Cup wins, by a very long way. When we were up against them, the 'Rock team was positively brimming with talent. Tony Forte and Mick Kelly were at half-back; Kelly would go on to get a soccer trial with Manchester United. The wings were the flying Peter Dee and professional-golfer-to-be John O'Leary. These guys, along with the mercurial Ben Underwood in the centre, presented us, and many others, with an impossible challenge.

Only our ferociously hard-tackling centre Owen 'Maxi' McAlinden gave them pause for thought. We knew that if he could get a couple of his 'specials' in early on, then we had a chance of keeping the score on the right side of respectable, but no more.

So my two years on the Belvedere Senior Cup team did not bring any success, with the last year in particular a great disappointment. Every October Belvedere travelled to play Heriot's School in Edinburgh – a trip no one wanted to miss. About a month before we were due to leave, my training had been curtailed by an accidental collision at the school's Jones' Road pitch, resulting in an ambulance trip and an overnight stay at the Mater Hospital, with a trapped sciatic nerve the diagnosis. But I was determined to travel, and probably rushed back to play too soon.

It's funny the things you remember clearly. The match against Heriot's was played at the beautiful Goldenacre pitch, which was, however, very wet from heavy overnight rain. I slipped and took a heavy fall, landing on an onrushing knee. It was a complete accident but I instantly knew I was in big trouble.

Everybody accepts pain differently and my admiration for those who cope with much, much worse is truly profound. I'd heard the word 'excruciating' before, without really understanding what it really meant. For me, this was truly excruciating. It was as if someone had fired a sharp, red-hot poker into my lower back, and that pain seared non-stop. For good measure, it then continued its merry way all the way down the length of my left leg.

I was transferred by ambulance from Goldenacre to an Edinburgh hospital, where significant damage to my lower back and a ruptured kidney was diagnosed, necessitating a move to another hospital in Glasgow. It was the loneliest moment of my life; the team went back to Dublin, and I hadn't any idea what would happen next. And with no mobile phones, texting or FaceTime, three coinbox telephones in the reception area, two of which were broken, were my only connection to home.

The Belvedere coach, Ger Brannigan SJ, had signed a form allowing the medics to do whatever was necessary. I wasn't supposed to see that 'transfer of power', but it only added to my interior terror, which I refused to show outwardly. Perhaps I should have.

For most of my stay, I was either high on whatever medication they fed me or I was sleeping, and the awful feeling of near-drowning never left me. I had reached my agony threshold and passing blood instead of urine was as unpleasant as it was frightening.

In Glasgow, the next bed to mine was occupied by the cut-up victim of a gang 'settling' and the razor blades had made quite a mess. I never got to find out what was going on, but there was an officer of the law sitting beside us, and another outside the door. Whenever I was awake, I felt it safer to pretend to be asleep.

After about a week, the blood ceased, and the doctors, deciding that it was safe for me to travel, checked me out. The trip home was agonising, every slight movement of the car on the way to the airport, and the flight itself, jolting my spine viciously. Nonetheless, knowing that family and friends would be waiting for me at the end of the journey kept me hobbling along.

That probably should have been the end of playing rugby for me, but with the impetuousness of youth, I returned in time for the Senior Cup the following spring. Potentially, we had a very good side, captained by Frank O'Brien, but we never really gelled. Keith Wood's father Gordon – also an Ireland and Lions front-row – had been asked to come in to help with the training and prepared us to play a forward-orientated game. It was called 'working the touch-line' – a strategy whereby our team would win a lineout, then the scrum-half or myself, as out-half, would kick it straight back into touch – and repeat, rinse and repeat, so that we'd keep gaining a few yards at a time.

It didn't really work for us, as it required an out-half of a different calibre to the one we had in that position, yours truly. I can claim, modestly, to have been a pretty good full-back, but not so at number 10. The latter was not my preferred position, but it was a case of needs must in that spring of 1967.

And so we arrived in Donnybrook to play the first round against Clongowes who, by contrast, had a tremendous kicker, Des Early, at out-half. We played poorly, but even so had a chance to draw level at the end and force a replay. Very late in the game, I hit a drop kick, left foot again, very similar to the one I had sent through the window in Dartry. On this occasion too the ball soared high, towards the posts but not through them, clipping the outside of the woodwork at the Bective end. That was that.

I did, however, have the great pleasure of playing with some of those 'Rock and Mary's boys on the Leinster schools team in that final year. The team was picked after a trial match, which the school had told me not to play in – their concern being that as we had gone out of the cup so early, we would not be fit enough. But myself and Bill Fegan – a doctor in the making – ignored this instruction, and took ourselves off to Donnybrook, both of us getting picked. When the Leinster lineup was published in the newspapers a few days later, the high command at Belvedere were in a dilemma: we had patently disobeyed a clear order, yet the fact that we'd been selected was a notable achievement for the school. Common sense prevailed and, after a ticking-off – as opposed to a more typical bashing – from Prefect of Studies Jack Leonard SJ, we all celebrated.

Having missed the clashes with Connacht and Munster through injury, I was now determined to play in the last interpro game of the season, against Ulster, who had not been beaten at this level for years. Our chances were deemed so slim that the Leinster branch Honorary Secretary, His Honour Judge Charlie Conroy, had promised that if we managed a victory, we could all keep our jerseys.

The match was won by the genius of that 'Rock three-quarter line, who bamboozled the Ulster defence. The pack supplied good ball and, at full-back, I was able to further worry the opposition by taking up a position just behind the centres. I didn't have much defending to do.

After the match, however, we found the esteemed judge stuffing the jerseys into a bin bag like a thief in the night – but we got them back from him without too much persuasion. It may not have been a Senior Cup medal but was a nice memento to finish what were great and enjoyable schoolboy rugby days.

The following season, by which time I'd finished school, my jersey had been filled by a much better and more natural out-half in the nimble-footed John Fegan. His ability, not to mention a different game plan ('Let's just enjoy it'), helped captain Ben Gormley and his team carry off the cup for Belvedere. A few years later, an even better out-half took to the stage, and Belvedere won two cups on the trot. The first of those, in 1971, was the rugby world's introduction to the sublimely elusive Ollie Campbell, who would pull on the green jersey of Ireland within five years.

Having made what I felt was a full recovery, I left for France in June 1967 as usual – by this time, I'd been able to secure a holiday job in Bordeaux, through some of my father's business contacts and those of my French 'assistant father' Jean Lawton, and the plan was to stay there for three months. It was manual, heavy work, helping to load and unload consignments along Bordeaux's Quai des Chartrons. I was the only pale-skinned Irishman rolling wine barrels to and from the boats, after arriving early every morning on my first motorised transport, an old and battered VéloSoleX. My back was holding up well and when harvest time came I went north of Bordeaux, into the Médoc, and worked the vintage at the Château Cantenac-Brown vineyard, owned then by the Lawtons.

I also made a few extra francs working for the Bordeaux

wine council. Nothing glamorous, however; it involved working with a crew in a lorry, travelling around the Médoc, hammering in wooden signposts at designated spots, to give passers-by directions to Château-this and Château-that. We'd get an early start and, by midday, we'd be ready to pull into a convenient roadside restaurant, joining all the other lorry crews at the communal table in the back.

There was a tradition whereby each of these guys had their own much-used knives, mostly for cutting baguettes with a practised, twisting motion. I had no such knife and toyed with the idea of buying a new one, but the thought of suddenly brandishing a gleaming new blade seemed worse than not having one at all. However, one day, just before we went in for lunch, my work partner tapped me on the shoulder. '*Pour toi* (for you),' he muttered, and handed me his own well-worn, spare knife. I knew then I had arrived.

When I returned home at the end of that summer to begin studying at University College Dublin, I had never been fitter or stronger, and my back felt as if it had never been hurt. So I was able to get a wonderful year of rugby in with the UCD freshman team. We were guided by coaches Michael Fitzsimons and Finbar Costello, with the simple prescription for play being: get the ball, pass and run. And then repeat.

There were many larger-than-life characters on that team, which included Arthur Cunningham, whose family were deeply involved with Shamrock Rovers, where he would later serve as chairman, and Jimmy Kinahan. Jimmy played scrum-half and would amble up to throw the ball into the scrum, his grandfather's shorts reaching to his knees – an approach which often lulled the opposition into a false sense of security. When the ball was won, however, he would scamper away from the base of the scrum at unexpectedly high speed, scoring and creating many tries. My old Belvedere teammate, Frank O'Brien, who'd captained our Senior Cup side the previous year, would step in for Kinahan from time to time, so the team was very well served in that number nine position.

The freshman team played, of course, against teams who were older and much heavier, so sometimes getting possession took quite a while. But if we were in touch going into the last 20 minutes, we knew we would have a lot more gas left in the tank than our opponents, and could pull off the required win. And win we did – sealing the league title that year. The final was played in Donnybrook, and it was the only time that I was ever on the winning team against 'Rock. Their back row included a certain Fergus Slattery, who would play with UCD the following season – and the rest, as they say, is history. It wouldn't be the last time our paths would cross.

In fact, we could have won the cup too, to make it a very rare double, but for – oh yes – a damn awful refereeing decision. We played that cup semi-final in dreadful conditions. Torrential rain turned the pitch into a quagmire and a gnarly, experienced Clontarf team put the ball up their collective jumper, we just couldn't get it. It looked like a no-score draw, but at least we'd get another chance in a replay. It wasn't to be, however – in the very late stages the man with the whistle decided we had collapsed a Clontarf maul, clearly a dreadful call. The penalty was kicked, and out we went, 0–3.

The following September, as many past pupils did, I joined Old Belvedere RFC in Ballsbridge. In pre-season, there was a trial match to see where everybody would likely fit. My immediate goal was the Second XV, and to challenge for the Firsts from there, but it was not to be.

At the Anglesea Road end of the main pitch, I shipped a fair but very heavy tackle as I made my way over the try line. I lay on the ground, not moving for about a minute, hoping against all hope that I was wrong. But no, I felt a terrible wrench, and that familiar back pain returned with a bang.

While not quite at the level of 'excruciating', there was no chance I could continue. I had the most ominous feeling as I walked off the pitch, a suspicion that my rugby days were done. My father was friends with expert orthopaedic surgeon Arthur Chance and, with little improvement a couple of months later, arranged for me to visit the good doctor. With this visit came very strong medical advice not to play again. Mr Chance explained very patiently and very clearly, using a model of skeletal vertebrae, what the conse-quences of a recurrence could be. It was a huge shock, but by now, having spent two long periods of being in intense pain, and unable even to bend down to put my shoes and socks on, I knew it was advice that could not be ignored.

To be told as a young man of 20 that it was now too much of a health risk for me to play the sport I loved was bitterly disappointing. It took a long, long time for the reality to sink in, and for me to accept that my rugby-playing days were over. It wasn't just that I had to give up the sheer physical enjoyment of the game, and all the excitement and camaraderie of being part of a team of like-minded people trying to achieve something. I was also having to let go of the hopes and dreams I'd had from a very young age, and the ambition to one day play for Ireland.

Perhaps my aspirations were beyond my abilities, but every part of me had been determined to give it a damn good try – no harm in aiming for the stars, as my father persistently drummed into all of us. As time went on, I'd see others of my generation who'd nurtured the same ambitions go on to achieve great things – Tony Ensor, for example, who'd come out of Gonzaga College at much the same time as I left Belvedere, and who made it to the very top in the number 15 jersey.

There was also the very important consideration that, in those days, rugby was still very much an amateur sport – and would indeed remain so until the 1990s. So while it was a huge passion of mine, even if I'd been able to 'go all the way', there was never any thought that it would or could be a full-time career. I was always going to have to find some other way of making a living. The fact that I was becoming increasingly interested in the French wine trade was some consolation, now that the rugby door was firmly closed behind me.

Being honest, and although I may not have admitted it at the time, there was also a modicum of relief involved. I followed all the rehab advice to the letter, with the very fortunate result that, to this day, I only experience occasional very mild back pain.

Chapter Three

21 December 1974

Blackrock v Bective Rangers in Lansdowne Road
(Leinster League final)

The game was very much in the melting pot on 52 minutes at 9–9. Three early Bective penalties had been replied to in kind by Blackrock, who now had the momentum and were chasing a lead.

Bective were pinned back close to their line and attempting to kick clear when I suddenly found myself unsighted on the wrong side of play. I assumed, as 'Rock's Jimmy Barrett gathered the ball before going over to score, that he had knocked it on and blew for a Bective scrum.

The looks Barrett and team-mate Fergus Slattery shot at

me were of sheer disbelief, they couldn't have faked it. I immediately knew I'd blundered.

It was a struggle to put the incident behind me for the rest of the game, and a lesson I'd have to learn the hard way.

• • •

When I was rolling barrels on the Quai des Chartrons in Bordeaux, I didn't expect to spend the next 20 years in the wine trade.

Having studied the making of wine all over France, including in Champagne, while spending my summers working in the export departments of several companies, I gradually became more involved in my father's business, taking it over in 1976. Thanks to the growth in consumption in Ireland around that time, I was able to increase business significantly. An English friend, Graham Street, was also learning the trade in France at the same time, and he would go on to become head wine buyer for the Army & Navy stores in London.

Charles Heidsieck was the leading brand of champagne in Ireland for many years; it was an independent, family-owned business, and three generations of my family have worked with them. Charles Heidsieck was also, for a large number of years, the in-house brand of Aer Lingus and would be served free on board to business travellers, who were then doling out over 400 Irish pounds for a return flight to London.

Jean-Marc Charles Heidsieck was, effectively, the export director of the company, with a brief of travelling the world to promote his wonderful product. He had a real love for Ireland as he had studied at Trinity College for several years, the only Frenchman in residence at the time. His next-door fellow-student was J.P. Donleavy, who completed his acclaimed novel *The Ginger Man* on a typewriter borrowed from 'The Champagne Man'. Jean-Marc had no trouble making friends, and was on the guestlist of many hostesses in Dublin, particularly those with eligible daughters, who, not unnaturally, saw the Frenchman as being a high-grade potential suitor. But he escaped the clutches of all and returned to France, where he met and married the stunning Nadine.

It was in Bordeaux and Reims that my love of good food really took off. Good fresh ingredients simply cooked, a bit like Rick Stein, were the order of the day. There was a cellar master who showed me a lot of the ropes and, on one memorable occasion, invited me to his house for Sunday lunch. Splendidly and aptly named Emile Potofeux, he collected me on his motorbike and, loaded with baguettes, we headed into the countryside. Emile lived with his wife in a small but very beautiful Hansel-and-Gretel-style cottage, and the smells coming from the kitchen when we arrived signalled what was to come. Home-made terrine followed by rabbit casserole, then cheese and dessert. All washed down with appropriate wine from bottles with no labels, obviously bartered. It remains one of the best meals I have been lucky enough to eat.

There is a lot of mythical nonsense spoken about the glamour of the wine trade. In reality, it's just a business like any other, although admittedly it has a tad more cachet than selling loo paper. You have to buy a product, sell it at a profit and get paid – often the hardest bit. I wish I could get back all the wasted hours I've spent chasing money from people who obviously thought we were in the banking business. One major supermarket group, H Williams, found itself in serious bother during a vicious price war, which eventually led to a change in legislation. Owned originally by Rolls-Royce-driving John Quinn and his family, I just about managed to get a cheque payment cleared in the bank, only days before the supermarket collapsed in 1987. Had I not, we might also have sunk.

Michael Quinn was the son of that owner and is very well remembered for his rugby exploits, playing for Dublin club Lansdowne for many years and winning 10 international caps as an excellent out-half. He notably scored a drop goal in Ireland's 26–21 win at Twickenham in 1974, on their way to the Five Nations title.

The ball popped out of the maul to England's Steve Smith but he was immediately pushed back over the goal line by Fergus Slattery, one part of a 'great green tidal wave', as evocatively described by Bill McLaren on the BBC's coverage. The nascent referee in me meant my eyes were drawn to the man in the red jersey of Wales, referee Meirion Joseph, wondering how much time he would add on.

Joseph indicated a scrum-five for Ireland. Quinn adjusted his socks before dropping into the pocket while the scum engaged and his half-back partner John Moloney spun the ball back to him. Under pressure, his kick was sliced slightly and clipped the right-hand post on its way over. The referee immediately blew for half-time, with Ireland 10–6 ahead and en route to a famous victory.

Myself and Quinn shared a pitch on a number of occasions, and there would have been many more caps for him but for Ollie Campbell, Paul Dean and Tony Ward who were also plying their trade in the '10' jersey around that same period.

One of the very necessary jobs in my early days running the family business was travelling the country visiting customers, and there were many good people I met along the way. But it wasn't a role I enjoyed much, although Waterford city was always an exception. The very elegant Laura Egan ran her own business there, as did the debonair Dayrell Gallwey who invented and produced Gallwey's Irish Coffee Liqueur, targeted at the American market.

But it was the visit to Henry Downes & Co. which never failed to be fun. Run at the time by Harry de Bromhead, who would appear out of the back room, dressed in polo shirt and jodhpurs, cheque in one hand and a new order in the other, always with time for a long sporting discussion, mostly about horse racing. If it was in the evening, Harry would bring me into the pub section of the premises and pour a couple of Downes' No. 9 whiskey that the company had been bottling since 1797.

My travels abroad more than compensated for the usually dreary drives around Ireland, with regular trips to France, Spain and Germany high on the agenda.

By a strange quirk of fate, I caught up with Harry again many years later on a holiday to France, where we shared many plates of oysters and crisp, white wine. His son, Henry, was trying to find his feet at that time as a trainer, and we all know by now how brilliantly he has managed his growing string of first-class racehorses, aided and abetted by the wonderful jockey Rachael Blackmore.

Yet no matter how much I was starting to enjoy the challenges and the perks of working in the wine trade, my passion for rugby was still very much there, and part of me still yearned to somehow be actively involved in the sport. It had been very hard to accept that my injury had put paid entirely to all my on-field hopes and dreams – and that the rugby door had been slammed shut behind me quite so finally. It was part of my father's upbeat philosophy in life that if one avenue closed, others would usually come into view – but, as I turned 20, I couldn't imagine what they could possibly be.

Then, the first Christmas after my injury returned, I had a conversation at my parents' house with another friend of my father's which completely changed my outlook. Noel

The Ref's Call

Hamilton 'Ham' Lambert had been one of the country's leading all-round sportsmen, playing both cricket and rugby for Ireland in the 1930s and '40s; he was also a final trialist for the national badminton team. Those were the days when you put away your rugby gear at the end of March and took out the summer sports equipment of cricket bats and tennis racquets. In his professional life, he was one of Dublin's leading veterinary surgeons.

In 1934, when Lambert was just 24 years old, a terrible knee injury in a club match at Lansdowne Road had put paid to his rugby-playing career (though he continued to play cricket for Ireland). But instead of accepting that it was the end of his days on the pitch, he decided he'd buy a whistle and take up refereeing. He excelled, and it wasn't long before he reached the top, regularly refereeing at Test level, including in the Five Nations. He was regarded as one of the best referees in the post-war era.

On this particular evening, 'Ham', who knew all about my devastating injury, took me aside for a chat. He told me his story and said that the world of refereeing was another rugby door that I should consider opening. Alternatively, he continued, I could just go on feeling sorry for myself, and fail to recognise a path which was there in front of me.

The chat brought up memories of an infamous incident I'd witnessed at Lansdowne Road seven years previously. It was December 1963, and Ireland had, in many people's eyes, beaten the All Blacks, but the scoreboard showed a loss to Wilson Whineray's touring New Zealanders by a single point, 6–5. Johnny Fortune of Clontarf Rugby Club had earlier crossed for an Irish converted try, but New Zealand had their noses just about in front thanks to a Kelvin Tremain try and a dubiously awarded Don Clarke penalty, as the match entered its final 10 minutes.

Ireland were not yet finished, and a towering cross-kick by Pat Casey was pounced on by Galway's Eamonn McGuire. Seated to the front of the old goal-line seats, I was far better positioned than the referee as McGuire touched down; it just had to be the winning score.

But the shrill blast of Mr H. Keenan's whistle was not to award the try, it was to deny it. The mystery deepened – and has never been solved – when, bafflingly, the referee awarded a scrum to the visitors, indicating a knock-on only he seemed to have seen. Ireland would have one more chance to claim a famous victory after engineering a drop at goal but Mick English's kick was mishit and that was that, game over. Whineray was later reported to have told his opposite number, Irish captain Ronnie Dawson, that the try should have been allowed.

It was to be a long, long wait for the first actual victory over New Zealand, and when it eventually came at Soldier Field in Chicago in 2016, 53 years had gone by since Keenan decreed that McGuire had knocked on.

'Even I could referee better than that man,' I remember telling my father as we left the ground. So I was very taken by both Ham's own story, and his obvious enthusiasm for refereeing. Being told I was feeling sorry for myself also struck a nerve – sulking was not part of our family creed.

Some months later, I was at my club, Old Belvedere, when the referee for a junior match failed to turn up, and, despite all of my protests, I was pressed into service. I would definitely have refused outright but for that recent chat with Lambert. I remember that no one had a whistle, and when eventually one was found, it was cracked and plastic. Together with a borrowed pair of boots, it was not a very stylish start. I'm not sure what the players thought of this initial performance, but my overriding emotion was one of sheer delight at actually being back running on a rugby pitch, even though it was a very different sort of involvement.

I discussed my plans with my father, who warned that it was anything but a given that I'd get very far; in fact, the chances of that happening were very slim, few made it. Jokingly, he apologised in advance that he wouldn't go to monitor my progress, as the greater likelihood was that I would fail, and that that would be hard to watch, even embarrassing. We laughed. I know he observed my progress proudly from a distance, but we didn't really ever dwell on it as time went by. There was no sense of having to prove anything to him; 'just do your very best' was an unspoken family motto and, with that sentiment fully ingrained, I set off to do just that.

I applied to join the Association of Referees, Leinster branch in 1969. The start was pretty informal – a 'laws of the game' book arrived in the post, together with a card appointing me to a few lower level matches. I took myself off to Elvery's Sports Emporium to arm myself with whistles, jerseys of various plain colours, shorts and socks. I think I only attended one referee meeting before taking charge of my first match, which was watched by an assessor, principally to confirm that at least I wasn't a danger to anyone.

It was the start of a long journey, which began with a state of unconscious incompetence – you don't know how bad you are. This must be particularly galling for the players, who know *exactly* how bad you are, while you whistle away, blissfully unaware.

By far the hardest part of the journey is the state of *conscious* incompetence – when you realise just how bad you are. You know the criticisms are justified, but you can't seem to find the solutions. Many who have started the journey find this bit very difficult, and throw in the towel at this point; it's not an enjoyable place to be.

Then, along comes conscious competence – you're getting better, and know what you should be doing, but you can be reactive, hesitant. But now the teams are starting to appreciate that you're making every effort, and are beginning to think that you might not be quite as bad as they had thought.

The final step is into the zone of unconscious competence, where you begin to do things by instinct, and it starts to become second nature to you. You're in automatic and the gears are changing by themselves.

All of this was ahead of me as I took charge of my first

matches, what could be called 'coarse' rugby friendlies. The Third and Second XVs' cups and leagues would follow if I proved capable. For example, long before the garda rugby team moved into their splendid premises in Westmanstown, they played in the Phoenix Park. It's nearly impossible to describe the merits of the pitch, which was uneven, lumpy and the supposed white marking lines were burnt into the ground, and, for good measure, not particularly straight. On arrival at this 'stadium', the first job was to help put up the goalposts, the holes for which were too wide, so we'd need to insert pieces of wood, or maybe a fallen branch, to keep them upright. If there was a high wind, the posts were in danger of coming down; if that happened all kicks at goal would have had to be taken at the other end.

The changing facilities were at least private, but that was as much as they had going for them. Missing panes of glass meant you could be certain of a chill wind blowing through the dressing rooms. Sometimes, the showers worked with a satisfactory flow of water; on other occasions they coughed and spluttered, yielding a mere trickle. But they were always cold, so I always left early to go home to a warm bath.

It would be a long time before I'd enjoy the comforts of Twickenham, where the head groundsman would serve the referee tea, asking how many sugars you took, as you relaxed in the steamy bath – at the perfect temperature – that had been prepared for you.

From the beginning of my refereeing career, I always

prided myself on being immaculately turned out, jersey perfectly ironed, shorts creased, boots so polished you could see your reflection in them. For those coarse rugby games, the players would turn up in dribs and drabs, and when they knew that at least thirteen had arrived – sure that would do – they'd start to get ready. They'd take out their kit, which had probably stayed in the bag since the previous match; sometimes, they didn't have matching jerseys, and there was generally an interesting and varied collection of socks, hardly the united colours of Benetton! As for the rugby . . . well, it could be termed robust, which would be the polite way of saying that the guards, in that context, were not for taking prisoners. Half-time would come and the oranges would be passed around, although a few players always preferred a smoke to topping up their vitamin levels.

Sallynoggin, just north of Dún Laoghaire on the south side of the city, was home to another pitch used by the Seapoint club. I remember a residents' right of way across it which, in general, was not used during play, but there were a couple of women who would notoriously insist on marching their prams across, so play would be held up as they availed of their legal rights. Seapoint have happily been ensconced in their 'new' grounds at Kilbogget in Killiney for many years now.

In the old days, Seapoint played the same brand of rugby as the guards and a match between these two clubs was always instructive. Genuinely so for an aspiring referee, with the opportunity to learn real and valuable lessons in controlling players and keeping a lid on things to prevent the pot from boiling over.

The pathway after that was senior club friendlies, at which point things started to get pretty competitive. And getting onto the group to referee at the Leinster Senior Club Cup, with all matches played at Lansdowne Road, was a very important step for an ambitious young man. Interpros and internationals were so far in the distance that they weren't even signposted, but they were, from the beginning, my well-defined targets.

From where I was, it looked a very long road ahead, and it would come with many challenges. I was refereeing players with whom I had played, and it took some of them a little time to take me seriously, while others were significantly older than me. It probably seemed odd to them but, in fairness, all of the clubs, without fail, gave me a warm welcome. Well at least my youth meant that, unlike some, I was able to keep up with play, even, if in the beginning, I wasn't much good.

All referees of that era had to overcome the dreaded assessment system which, perhaps inevitably, was laced with subjectivity. Some assessors were excellent, fair and helpful. Others, just like referees, were not so hot. Some were known for always writing severe reports, and it was very frustrating to spot one of these patrolling the touchline.

After two seasons at junior level, things started to move on apace, and during the 1971–72 season – sooner than I expected, to be honest – notification arrived of my first senior club match, St Mary's RFC v Trinity College at Fortfield Road in Terenure. The former were determined to make things very difficult for the students, the match was physical and quickly bordered on getting out of control.

The kick-off was quickly followed by a mass brawl, and skirmishes continued to break out during the first half. One fight calmed here, another starting there, with as much blood flowing as there was sweat. I was at my wits' end, and realised that I'd have to send someone off. Before that happened, I caught the eye of a tall, rangy Mary's player.

'Any chance you could give me a hand here, this is not going to end well,' I said.

He didn't reply, but despite his look of incredulity, he did have a quick word with his team-mates. It was like someone had flicked a light switch; the trouble subsided straightaway. This was my first encounter with broad-caster, writer and rugby pundit George Hook.

After the match, I thanked him and he growled back that it was the first time a referee had ever asked him to do anything other than to go back 10 metres. The two referee assessors were delighted, declaring that, while there were a few technical issues that needed attention, my control had been of an unexpectedly high standard. Job done, then – albeit with a little help.

By now, I was also refereeing schools rugby. Given the prestige of the tournaments, Senior Cup matches are prized appointments for any referee in all four provinces every spring, and the atmosphere is inevitably electric, with crowds reaching tens of thousands for the final. But these matches come with a proviso: don't make a mistake. Far preferable to do that in Twickenham, Murrayfield or Cardiff than in a key schools match. As recently as last year, believe it or not, my great mate Terry Hayden laughingly told me that his wife Joan had been instructed by a very good friend of hers to get him to speak to me: 'Tell your husband to say to that referee friend of his, we have not forgotten.'

I imagine that she would have been talking about an epic Leinster Schools Senior Cup struggle between hot favourites St Mary's and Clongowes. These two schools rarely fail to provide dynamic fare, and with the stands in Donnybrook rocking, Mary's had a good half-time lead, 19–3 if memory serves. But Clongowes never go away and never give in. They started to claw their way back, and when they dotted down a last-minute try in the corner, they knew the conversion would win it for them. The kicker was tense as he set up the ball and stepped back. As he did so, he slipped in a small groove that used to run down along the fencing on that side of the pitch. Picking himself up, he smiled, all the tension gone – and perhaps he didn't realise it but, at that moment, I knew the kick would surely split the posts. And it did.

With no idea that I was going to be blamed for the defeat, I trotted happily off the pitch and soon found out what was what. Now, there was absolutely no nastiness, but as I went the short distance to the Bective pavilion, I was left with no doubt at all as to the feelings of parents and 'old boys'. My own view was that Mary's had, with that substantial lead, taken their foot off the pedal, and their opponents had upped the ante in a very big way. But it just showed how very high emotions run, and it is still exactly the same today, if not more so.

In the men's game, the Leinster Senior Club Cup was the foremost competition, and was played on successive Saturdays, with a double header at Lansdowne Road each day. When two teams would finish and run off at the old Wanderers pavilion, two more would immediately take to the pitch from the Lansdowne clubhouse end. With matches very rarely running much more over the allotted time, it was easy to synchronise. Imagine trying to do that in professional rugby, with its many stoppages leading to halves which commonly can be fifty minutes long or more.

As a kid, I had regularly gone to watch these matches, and now, in a very different role from the one I'd anticipated, I was starting to become involved myself. If not whistling, there were appointments to assist. Given their integral nature in today's game, it's very hard to believe that the assistant referees, then referred to as touch judges, had no job apart from marking the position of touch and signalling whether kicks at goal went over or wide. Even if they were aware of foul play, they couldn't interfere, which led to some interesting goings-on. After all, if a player wanted to dole out some punishment to an opponent all he had to do was to check out where the referee was first, knowing full well that the touch judges could say nothing, even if they saw a punch.

But these were the most valuable of lessons; working with much higher level referees was a real learning curve. Heck, I even touch-judged for Kevin Kelleher on occasion, how could I not learn? Watching them closely as they went about their business, learning from their decision-making and their communication, both the good and the bad, was invaluable.

And, of course, some of the things I saw at close quarters I did not appreciate. There were referees who I felt were over-severe and very penalty-punitive in their approach. I determined quickly that that would not be my way of working.

Of perhaps even more value was watching them before kick-off, how they interacted with players – usually in a matter-of-fact way, but light and relaxed humour was also part of it. These were key, competitive matches, and it was important to find the right balance; it was second nature to a man like Kelleher. Teams always seemed particularly happy to see Dave Burnett or John West, they brought an affability and a quiet wit to the pre-match proceedings. Without for a second wishing to copy their personalities, I could see that their player-friendly attitude was very much the way to go.

In one of my early cup matches, I was left with no option

but to send off a player for what was a very nasty boot to the head of an opponent. I was fortunate to have just changed position and so it happened right in front of me. But the charges were very forcibly denied, which was unusual; the norm in rugby is for players to accept the referee's decision. However, the very eminent Jack Coffey of the Lansdowne club, who served a term as IRFU president, was seated in the stand. He'd had a very clear view, which, with no prompting, he later confirmed in writing, and that put the issue beyond any doubt.

Coffey, also a fine yachtsman, had skippered his sloop *Meg of Muglins* on an epic three-month Atlantic crossing, over and back, with the whole voyage covering nearly 8,000 miles. After setting sail, they met the most raging of seas and high winds, so it was a trip not for the faint-hearted, but it was successful. In his own account of it all, he talks of 'contentment won by strenuous endeavour', which it most certainly was. Clearly made of stern stuff, his endorsement of my decision was prized.

It's a referee's obligation to learn from past mistakes and poor performances but not to overly dwell on them in the moment. I was lucky to learn that lesson early on, in the 1974–75 Leinster League final at Lansdowne Road – Bective Rangers, captained by future IRFU President Louis Magee, v Blackrock. My progression had been coming along nicely and I was very happy to have been appointed to what was a high-profile fixture. But, momentarily unsighted during the game, as 'Rock's Jimmy

The Ref's Call

Barrett gathered an awkward rolling ball before crossing, I ruled that he had knocked on, and blew. On reflection, he had not, he had legitimately charged down a clearing kick before picking up.

My error was abundantly clear from the faces of the Blackrock players. Rather than the look of protest at a debatable decision, theirs was of such sheer disbelief that it was clear they were in the right.

That incorrect call stuck in the centre of my brain for the rest of the match, and certainly affected my performance. Later on, I threw my kitbag in the car boot and slammed it down hard. That was the first time the car bore the brunt of my frustration, and it wouldn't be the last.

While the decision didn't impact the result, with Blackrock claiming the title, as I got home to my Terenure flat, the late-night sports report on the radio told me: '. . . and to make matters worse, after that error the referee blew the whistle at every possible opportunity'. I sighed and thought there'd be more of it in the newspapers the next day. And indeed there was.

No matter what code, all referees have to learn to put their mistakes behind them, and to find a mechanism to do so. It's not easy, but if an error continues to prey on your mind, then nothing is more certain than that more errors will follow. It's not as simple as just saying something to yourself, you have to create a strong mental image that 'deletes' the mistake. This enables you to carry on as if it never happened, and so the temptation to even things up is non-existent. Going down that road is like trying to level the legs of a three-legged stool. Time enough to revisit it, and the reasons, later on. Trust me, there'll be plenty of people to remind you.

My own mental image was to slam a perceived mistake into the darkness of the boot of my car. No matter where I was in the world, my car would always be 'mentally' parked just behind the stand.

Some referees used the car-boot method, others invented different techniques of their own. The wastepaper basket or the fire would work for many, while others saw a mistake to be just like stalling the car – restarting the engine being the key to putting the error behind them.

There were of course occasional disasters, the final of the Leinster Senior Cup in 1977 being one of them. Tommy Kearns had given exceptional and long service to the game, and was a very good referee, though with a tendency to be somewhat officious. He would often give the most marginal of crooked-in scrum decisions, and as these were full penalties at the time, worth three points, those calls could often determine the result of the game.

Kearns, of St Mary's RFC, was coming to the end of his career, and it was decided to give him the final, perhaps as a going-away present. It was Terenure v University College Dublin, and the match was decided in UCD's favour by a very questionable decision: Terenure's Brendan 'Boo-Boo' Lynham lined up a late straight penalty kick on the UCD 22 to put his side ahead. He didn't chip it, but instead hit it very hard; the ball slammed into one post and ricocheted over to the other, travelling at high speed. It then seemed to disappear. Spectators behind the posts, who were expecting the ball to go over their heads, later said that they'd lost sight of it completely.

Touch judges David Burnett and Andrew Mather, the only people who could know, had seen that the ball had passed just inside the second post as it shot across the face of the goal, so they signalled that the kick was good. To their astonishment, they watched as Kearns disallowed the kick and awarded a drop-out to UCD. Burnett, who had run back to halfway for the anticipated restart, returned to the 22, where he outlined to the referee the trajectory, and the route, the ball had taken. Kearns, very unwisely and disastrously, contradicted him.

Later that evening, the outraged losers had repaired to their clubhouse in Terenure, and Kearns, by now realising the error of his ways, decided, albeit foolishly, to travel up there to make his peace, accompanied by his wife, Sheila. His assistants and their wives went too, in moral support. It was all done with the very best of intentions, but the timing could not have been worse. It was forgivable that they weren't welcomed with open arms, but drink did some irate talking, and also a little bit of pushing and shoving, forcing the couple into a hasty retreat.

This incident could have been blown into something huge, but wisdom prevailed in Terenure the next morning. The president and several senior committee members arrived at the Kearns' home, heartfelt apologies were made, accompanied by flowers, and were accepted. Flowers too for the wives of the touch judges.

While Kearns was undoubtedly a good referee, in my view, then and now, he was not at all the equal of either of his two fellow club members Vinny McGovern and Matt Gilsenan.

Old Wesley RFC had a marvellous team in the mid-1970s, coached by Ian Cairnduff, the proprietor of Dublin's foremost delicatessen and wine emporium, Smyths of the Green. They were always very well prepared and, assisted by a sprinkling of international players in Phil Orr, Alan Doherty and Eric Campbell, made the Leinster Senior Cup final in 1975. Their opponents were St Mary's, a very strong team with Tom Grace on the wing, Johnny Moloney at scrum-half, and Denis Hickie and Sean Lynch in the forwards. As he had at school, Henry Russell-Murphy, while not an international, very effectively partnered Moloney at out-half.

I had no idea the appointment to handle the final was coming my way, so it was quite some surprise, considering it was only my sixth season, not to mention my poor call in the league decider. But that had only been one game, and my other performances across the season had obviously been noted.

The match was drawn 6–6, and went to a replay, which tradition dictated retained the same referee. Mary's won that by a solitary point, 10–9, thanks to a Tom Grace kick from the touchline; he had scored all their points in both matches. The losing coach, Cairnduff of the Green, was the first to shake my hand. Later, another handshake came my way – from my father, who'd been proudly in attendance at both games, his earlier joke about never watching me referee a source of amusement for us both.

After that 1975 final, I started to dream again, thinking that the impossible might not be so impossible after all.

Chapter Four

9 October 1976

Gloucester v Harlequins in Kingsholm
(Annual friendly match)

Nobody had bothered to mention to me that Harlequins was a huge match for Gloucester – the men from the Forest of Dean relishing the opportunity to rough up their visitors from London.

I was also completely unaware of the hostile atmosphere the crowd in the famous 'Shed' would whip up.

It was undoubtedly the worst performance of my career so far – I was shocking.

And when you're not able to get even an ounce of enjoyment out of it, time drags – I thought we'd never get as far as half-time.

• • •

The Ref's Call

Despite my progress through the refereeing ranks, not everything was plain sailing.

At a very early stage in my career – too early, in hindsight – I was sent to Kingsholm in the English West Country, which was home to a very uncompromising and tough team, Gloucester. The visitors that day were Harlequins, a fixture always highlighted on the calendar by the hosts.

We glean from our dictionaries that in English pantomime Harlequins are mute characters supposedly invisible to clown and pantaloons. They are also a small breed of spotted dog and a northern species of duck as lesser-known meanings, the match programme read. *But we in the world of rugby know only too well there is nothing burlesque, ludicrous, canine or duck-like about the famous Harlequins, who we cordially welcome to Kingsholm, though they might, with their spectacular style of open play, almost appear invisible on occasions.*

In reality, the welcome was far from cordial and it was open play rather than the visiting players that was nigh on invisible. The huge error I made that day was in overplaying advantage early on. Before I knew it, there were off-the-ball incidents breaking out all over the place.

During half-time, I realised that there was only one way to deal with it – to allow zero advantage. Instead, I played a merry tune on the whistle; Lord knows how many penalties there were in that second half. The crowd had every right to be as displeased as they sounded but, at the time, it was pretty harrowing stuff.

At the time, referees were assessed by a rather quaint and often incomprehensible letter system, A to E. I came out with a D from that game – on reflection, that was probably generous. But, as is the case with all referees, I didn't need an assessment to tell me how I had performed.

Having been moving up the ladder quickly, that performance sent me sliding back down the snake. And so it should have.

I spent a miserable evening drowning my sorrows over a lonely meal. Having tried to get the bill several times, I just left without paying, such was my annoyance with life and all things rugby. Walking back towards my hotel, the terrifying noise of a police siren came up fast behind me. For a moment, I really thought I was about to be arrested, and the huge relief when it sped past persuaded me to return post-haste to the restaurant and pay up. Whatever about a poor performance finishing me off, a night in the clink would certainly have done so.

Part and parcel of developing as a referee was travelling around the country, to referee matches in the other provinces. And as I was appointed to games outside Leinster, there were similar experiences. A match in Ballina, County Mayo, nearly finished me off. The club's pitch was unplayable following a week of continuous rain and it looked like I'd be turning my car around, my journey wasted. However, there was another pitch, one that I was reliably informed never flooded, though nobody mentioned why not. And so we changed and drove out of town, fully togged out, while it was still raining cats and dogs.

Eventually, we turned off the main road and drove up what was little more than a track and, there it was, the pitch that always drained. Of course it did, it sloped at about a 30-degree angle from one touchline to the other. Not only that, the playing surface had more in common with a cattle field than a rugby pitch. The heavy rain continued and, by half-time, having been exposed to the dreadful elements for 40 minutes, we were soaked to the skin. Sheltering for the break under nearby trees, we didn't even have the traditional half-time oranges for comfort: they'd been forgotten.

After a second half in similar conditions, we went back to town in a state of near hypothermia and I was starting to wonder why on earth I kept giving up my free time to do this – why did anyone? I decided I would shower and change, have a sandwich and head back to Dublin, defeated. Maybe I could learn to hit a golf ball.

But the Ballina club president, the ebullient Sean Murphy, intervened and invited me and others back to his home for a wonderful spread, accompanied by liberal servings of the alcohol of our choice. My journey home didn't start until late the following morning, by which time I was thinking that maybe things weren't so bad after all.

In Munster, it was sometimes necessary to convince the assessors that you had done better than they thought. The post-match chat was nearly as important as how you'd actually performed. Noel Moore and Michael Reddan were very good Munster assessors and sometimes they worked as a team. Their way of breaking bad news gently was to ask the dreaded question, 'How do you think you did yourself?' When those words were uttered, you knew it was going to be a long, tricky discussion. Reddan had been a fine referee before illness struck, so he turned his hand to assessing. His observation skills were good, but he often used one of my least-favoured expressions in the whole of the English language: 'I don't disagree with you.'

The club rivalries in Limerick are particularly legendary, and one of my favourite memories came when refereeing at Thomond Park later in my career. It was January 1992, the heyday of the All Ireland League, and Shannon and Garryowen were locked in a typically epic derby battle with over 14,000 spectators shoehorned into the yet-to-be-developed stadium.

The atmosphere was hot, with play around the Shannon 22, as I gave a very speculative advantage to Garryowen. Possession wasn't great for the men in light blue, but something in my head made me think, *Let's see if there's anything on here.*

What transpired to be 'on' went way beyond what I expected. A dummy and a deft side-step created a line-break followed by a scorching run to the try line, a magnificent score. To my astonishment, that was all done by the still teenage Garryowen hooker, Keith Wood. He was already announcing his prowess to the rugby world, and here was a new trick.

Unsurprisingly, his first cap of a wonderful career, which saw him crowned the inaugural World Player of the Year in 2001, came just two years later during Ireland's tour of Australia.

His selection for that Ireland debut provided something of a dilemma for another big local rival of Garryowen, as Wood was to be propped by two great stalwarts of Young Munster RFC, Peter Clohessy and John 'Paco' Fitzgerald. A carefully worded message of congratulations was faxed to Wood, advising that: 'The lads will look after you, but only on foreign soil. Normal business will resume in Limerick.'

Wood wouldn't have had it any other way and, sure to their word, when the two teams met the following October, there were himself and Clohessy knocking seven bells out of each other. I can vouch for it, I was the man in the middle that day as well, having to remind them that, as I'd heard they'd both been picked to play for the Barbarians the following week, they might prefer if I didn't have to send them off.

The train journey home from Munster assignments was also always tremendous fun, no matter how well, or not, you had done. The referees leaving Cork were responsible for getting things set up, reserving the seats for those who had been reffing in Limerick and who, after getting the connecting train, would board at Limerick Junction. More importantly, they would make sure that enough steaks were put aside in the kitchen, and with dinner not served until after the Junction, they got the red wine and beer flowing. Not a word of a lie, that train served the best and juiciest meat, cooked to your taste by the on-board chef.

Years later, international referee Brian Stirling was waiting on that platform, having whistled a match at Young Munster, and was slightly alarmed when he was approached by a supporter, decked out from head to foot in the famous black and gold colours, bottle of beer in hand, swaying slightly. But he needn't have been concerned, it was just a simple rugby question, about whether Owen Doyle had retired or not. When Stirling replied that, yes, Doyle had just retired, the swaying supporter politely informed him, 'Well, then, you're now the worst referee in Ireland.'

The journey was always hilarious, and we were often joined by future High Court President Ricky Johnson, the keenest of rugby supporters. That most learned judge, a raconteur par excellence, regaled us with stories of his days at the bar and on the bench, and neither was he left behind when the discussion turned to rugby law. As much as we promised ourselves it wouldn't – it invariably did.

The arrival into Heuston Station always came too soon, and those travelling on to Belfast via Connolly had still some way to go, but were mostly sleeping like babes for that final leg of the trip.

On my own travels to Ulster, I always felt that there was a very fair approach from the province's assessors. Jim

Irvine, who would later travel the globe on International Rugby Board (IRB – now known as World Rugby) assessment duties, read the game very well, and felt his role was to assist as well as assess. He would go on to make a long and valuable contribution to the IRFU referee committee.

Alan Sturgeon was of the same ilk, very knowledgeable and reasonable; it was always a pleasure to see him turn up at matches. Popular with colleagues and players alike, Sturgeon had just been appointed to the interprovincial panel in Ulster when he was picked to referee Munster v Argentina at Thomond Park during the Pumas' 1973 tour. For a first representative assignment, it was really throwing the referee in at the deepest of ends. With the visitors well versed in the dark arts, and the hosts no shrinking violets themselves, this was a match which was bound to be full-on. Little did anybody know just how full-on that autumn day would turn out to be.

Understatingly described as 'tempestuous' on the history section of Munster's website, Paul MacWeeney's match report from the following day's *The Irish Times* better captures what Sturgeon had to contend with:

There has been many a lusty battle at Thomond Park since Munster first entertained overseas touring sides in 1948. But the first appearance in Europe of a representative Argentina team provided a really ugly display of vicious use of boot, shoulder and fist and on four occasions there were punch-ups in which half the players of each side were involved. Yesterday the home player who had the ball in his grasp was often in less danger than the team-mate who had passed it to him, and the number of times a player was felled when the play had moved some distance from him made this an unpleasant business to watch.

The *Irish Independent*'s Colm Smith went even further in his report:

If what we saw at Limerick's Thomond Park yesterday is indicative of Argentina's attitude to rugby football, the world of sport would be better off if they confined their activities to South America. I have never seen, on any sporting field, a more vulgar approach to tackling, a more blatant diligence to that unsporting phrase 'if you can't get the ball, get the man'.

It really was a brutal battle, the air was acrid with ill-temper, and, of course, with no TMO to assist in sorting things out, the players knew that just one pair of eyes was surveiling matters. It was an impossible task, simply unrefereeable. Sturgeon spent most of the match trying to put out fires; as soon as one was quenched, another started. The final score of 12–12 was almost forgotten amid the mayhem.

Following this, the powers that be unfairly decided that

Sturgeon had issues with control, which was like saying that Field Marshal Montgomery had issues at El Alamein. So he never made the final step. Nobody stopped to think that, compared to this match, a Five Nations fixture would have seemed like a walk in the park.

I did have some good fortune in Ulster club matches, particularly one foul-weather day when Queen's University played Malone in the early 1980s. The rain had teemed down all morning, as it had all night. While it was easing, as I arrived at the ground, I doubted the pitch would be playable, but I was told not to worry. We ran out and practically waded across several pitches, before arriving at a veritable oasis. Queen's had installed one of the first all-weather 'Prunty' pitches, and it had just come into operation.

While most matches across the province were called off that day, we had a great time; the ball was run by both teams, fast and furious. I didn't have much to do, and the assessor liked what he saw. He was Brian Baird who, in his dulcet tones, read the news on UTV for many years.

Journeys to Belfast during the Troubles were not without their own particular difficulties, and some of these trips could be quite worrisome. But referees continued to travel, even though we were nearly always alone. We would often go by car, but the Dublin–Belfast road, pre-motorway, was a nightmare, even getting out past the airport to Swords was an absolute drag. There was the option of the train but, all too often, there would be a warning that a bomb was on the tracks and the train would stop at Dundalk, where a bus was waiting to take its passengers into Newry, where we would join another train for the final leg of the journey.

I was leaving Dublin for Ulster's home ground of Ravenhill very early one Saturday morning to referee the curtain-raiser to the senior match of the day, a visit from Munster. With traffic reported as heavy, I decided on the train but, just as we were boarding, one such warning came through. It became clear that I wouldn't make the early kick-off time, so I put through a call from a phone box to say that, as there was no chance at all of my arriving in time, there was no point in travelling.

Years later, after I had refereed a senior interpro at the same ground, an old gentleman tottered over to me to say that he thought I hadn't been as bad as the last time he saw me – you have to love them, these compliments. As I thanked him he asked, 'What happened to that other Doyle fellow, who refused to come up here because of the Troubles?' I pondered his question for a moment before telling him that I believed that particular Doyle had emigrated to Australia. 'Damn good job, that,' he muttered as he tottered off again.

Long before the invention of the sat nav, travelling by car brought its own difficulties for me. My sense of direction is such that I would get lost going home from the shops, so anytime I arrived in Belfast there remained the very tricky business of finding the hotel. And, for some reason I have never quite figured out, I was usually billeted in the Europa Hotel, infamous as the most bombed hotel in Europe.

The Ref's Call

Dining there on Friday evenings was always interesting; the food was good but, several times, it was unnerving to be asked to move to a different table because of a bomb scare in the vicinity. The army would arrive at the scene, cordon everything off and then manoeuvre a robot down the street into the suspect building, usually a pub. Despite being attacked many times, suffering explosions on countless occasions, the hotel remained standing, and that is something of a miracle. I travelled to Belfast mostly during the 1970s, '80s and early '90s, during which there were at least 36 such attacks.

Normally, on the day of an interprovincial match, the referee stayed over, attended the post-match dinner and headed home the next day. But on one occasion, I had to be home early on Sunday morning, so as I drove out of Belfast it was approaching midnight and pitch dark. At least there wouldn't be any traffic, I thought, but it turned out there would be something else. The roads were eerily deserted as I approached the border, with only occasional moonlight as the clouds scudded overhead.

Suddenly, there was something ahead, or rather somebody; a lone, heavily camouflaged soldier was waving me to a halt. As I stopped, the car was immediately surrounded by his fellow troopers; all of these guys seemed to be about 16 years of age, their machine guns shaking in their hands.

I was terrified as I explained who I was, but that had to be verified by a look into my kit bag which was in the boot of the car. The officer very carefully opened the boot and

I unzipped the bag, but I was pulled away as I went to reach into it. This all went on for what seemed like hours as he satisfied himself that I was genuine but, in reality, it was probably no more than 15 minutes. Suddenly, they disappeared into the hedgerows, with a warning that there was a lot of IRA activity about that night.

All the way back to Dublin, I kept seeing shadowy figures in the ditches; maybe it was my imagination or perhaps it was not. This was several years before the high-profile kidnapping of John O'Grady in 1987, and his brutal treatment at the hands of his INLA captors. John had been a classmate of mine at St Conleth's and we'd played rugby together on the under-12s team. The fact that I knew him personally meant the incident resonated strongly.

That danger had also been highlighted in horrific fashion earlier in 1987, when Ulster players Nigel Carr, Philip Rainey and David Irwin were caught up in the bomb blast of the IRA's assassination of Lord Justice Maurice Gibson and his wife Lady Cecily. The players were travelling together to training in Dublin ahead of that year's inaugural Rugby World Cup (RWC) in Australia and New Zealand, on the route I had driven many times. The lord justice was returning home to Northern Ireland via the Dún Laoghaire ferry following a visit to Britain. The force of the blast hurled the judge's car into Irwin's at what was estimated to be over 120 miles per hour.

Incredibly, all three players survived, with Irwin and Rainey actually taking their places on the plane to Australia the following month. But the injuries sustained by Carr meant he would, sadly, never play again. Both atrocities brought home the very real dangers of being in the wrong place at the wrong time back in those dark days.

In all my time undertaking those trips, I never once thought of not going; the whole ethos of Irish rugby is that it is played in all four provinces and all of these contribute to make up the Irish team. It is without any doubt whatsoever a huge force for good on this island, and the fact is that a team from the Republic alone wouldn't be nearly as good as the one which embraces everybody. I wouldn't have missed the hospitality and the friendships I have made north of the border for the world, and, whatever it is about rugby, I have never come across an extreme, unacceptable view on the very difficult political questions that continue to be posed in Ulster.

Chapter Five

3 October 1981

Llanelli v Neath in Llanelli
(Local derby)

It was infringement after infringement and, 15 minutes in,
the whistle had barely left my lips.

At yet another break in play, the wonderful Wales and
Lions centre, Llanelli captain Ray Gravell, came over to me.

I braced myself for what was coming next, but was very
pleasantly surprised when he simply said, 'Keep at it,
young man – they'll soon give up and we'll get a game of
rugby.'

Bolstered by this very timely and supportive intervention, I
upped the ante, and gave it, so to speak, both barrels.

As quickly as a rainy day in Ireland can turn to sun, the

aggro evaporated, and we ended up getting a half decent game of rugby.

•   •   •

Having now gained valuable experience refereeing across Ireland, everything was going well. However, I then hit a few serious performance rocks that proved to be a very tricky setback, and were nearly my undoing.

In those days, each province announced a panel of three interprovincial referees each season. That group of 12 got all the major matches within Ireland and qualified to go on exchange matches with the other Five Nations unions. To be outside that dozen meant that there were no representative matches available for a referee.

I'd first nailed down a spot within that group in 1975–76 and felt I had acquitted myself well, both in Ireland and on my occasional trips across the water. But I found it very annoying that the assessment system was completely subjective, solely based on opinion. Often, referees didn't feel that they'd had a fair break from their assessor.

As the 1979–80 season was dawning, I was looking forward to more of those exchange games. Instead, I got a call one evening from my old headmaster at Conleth's and Leinster branch President Kevin Kelleher, in his capacity as chairman of selectors, with the news that I had been dropped. He told me that I shouldn't worry, there was always a way back, but considering that the decision put me outside the top 12, worried was precisely how I felt. Damned worried, in fact. I remember thanking Kelleher for his call, before throwing the phone at the wall and opening a bottle of wine. I reckoned that I had probably only one season, at the most two, to regain the lost ground, before I'd become another 'yesterday's man'.

It may sound completely an idle claim, but when I performed poorly, my first instinct was to try and work out why things had not gone according to plan, and to leave absolutely no stone unturned in doing so, to make sure that it didn't happen again. I never crawled into a corner and worried about it or, worse, tried to cover it up. It seemed to me that finding the solution was the thing to do, and it was certainly the most positive. It resulted in always having the necessary confidence and drive to continue, rather than, at any stage, to consider throwing in the towel. Confidence is a funny thing, it can quickly turn to overconfidence, and then arrogance is just a step away. When that happens, any arbiter, in any sport, is on a downward curve.

All the best referees are strong psychologically, and there's no doubt that my strength came from another family motto: 'regret nothing but learn from everything'. And learning from mistakes is just about the most important thing you can do. Sure, you must apologise for errors along the way, but regretting the mistake and overfocusing on it will surely prevent fixing it for the next time.

The Ref's Call

You can sort of encapsulate that into a rugby goal-kicker who misses a shot he'd have been expected to get. A similar kick comes along in the next match. He won't have spent the intervening moments regretting his miss, beating himself up over it; rather, he'll have worked out why it went wrong and be confident that he'll strike it properly this time around. Golfers must be the same, particularly when they've just driven into the water. As they line up the shot again, their mental picture must not be to visualise the last attempt splashing down, but rather the ball rolling onto the green.

In those days, there were no development courses, you were just told how well or badly you'd done, so it was essential to create self-help tools, such as my own 'walking the beach' technique, to sort things out.

So I forced my disappointment to one side and replaced it with a determination that my absence would not be for long. There was obviously a reason for my deselection, and I pondered the likely causes.

The brilliant rugby tactician, Ireland and Lions prop forward Ray McLoughlin had politely queried a few scrum decisions I had given against him when playing for his club Blackrock. So I called him up and we sat down together. I also sought out Leinster and Trinity scrum guru Roly Meates.

There was absolutely nothing that these two men didn't know about scrummaging. The body angles, the foot positions, how to pressurise, how to take pressure and much more besides. Up to then, my scrum decisions had been well-meant guesstimates, but now, with essentially a master's degree in the art of scrummaging, I knew that I would be so much better in this area and would be able to talk to front-rows in their own language. Meates, very kindly, would remain as my scrum advisor throughout my career.

Next, I went along to watch matches at Lansdowne Road whenever I wasn't refereeing myself. Perched in the stand, looking down at play panoramically, I saw things both good and not so good, and learned from both. The two very positive elements that were really noticeable, and became trigger words for me, were anticipation and positioning. Neither can survive without the other and, many years later, I would introduce a form of equine dressage for referees, to assist them with these key needs.

There is no doubt at all that the year after I had been dropped, my performances improved immeasurably. It was the off-field work and study that had enabled it.

Armed with this additional knowledge, I regained the interpro panel position the following season. Eventually, those exchange matches started to come my way once more, although they posed a threat of a different kind – again assessor subjectivity could prevail.

Some of these matches had distractions that had nothing to do with rugby. In 1980, I travelled to Exeter to referee an England trial match, South v South-West. I was picked up at the airport by an apparently very genial Devon farmer and local clubman, and we headed towards town and my hotel. At least that's what I thought. As he turned off the main road, he explained that he lived in a very nice farm-house, so it'd be much more enjoyable for me if I stayed with him and his good lady wife. I could already smell the home-cooking, and imagine the accompaniment of the best locally crafted cider.

However, on arrival he showed me to an absolutely freezing room, and everything went downhill from there as he outlined the order of play. If I needed something to eat, there was a nice pub about five miles down the road, he'd give me a lift if I wanted, just knock on the sitting-room door. An hour later I did so, and looked into the most comfortable of sitting rooms, fire blazing.

After I'd finished a much-needed delicious cottage pie, plus some of that cider, plus a few warming hot whiskeys to finish off (hardly the ideal pre-match preparation, but it was that or pneumonia), I called up my friendly farmer and he came to collect me. The next morning, the worst farm-house breakfast was presented; also presented was the bill for B&B, plus a hefty taxi service charge. I paid up, got him to drive me into town, and went to bed in the hotel room which had originally been reserved for me. That few hours' sleep in a warm bed were essential, but still I remember little about the match itself.

Another England trial match was allocated to me some time later, and I remember leaving the field thinking, *Well, that wasn't too bad at all.* On arrival in the bar post-match, I sought out my assessor, former England international Peter Brook, but he was nowhere to be found. As the crowd in the bar dwindled a few hours later, I enquired again if anybody had seen him. 'Oh, he left the ground with 20 minutes to go,' I was told, which was obviously very uncomfortable news. In the heel of the hunt, when his assessment reached the IRFU, it wasn't too bad at all, and included a short explanation that he'd had to leave early so as not to be late for dinner and the theatre that evening.

Next, it was off to Paris, and a match at Racing Club's then home ground, the 'old' international pitch at Stade Colombes. Picked up at my hotel three hours before kick-off, I was driven out to the Bois du Boulogne where Racing had a splendid tennis club, equipped with an excellent dining room. This was my first, but most definitely not my last, experience of trying to extract my French minder/driver from his lunch, and subsequent cognac, so that we might get to the ground with some time to spare. Eventually, we left, and after the first of many scary drives across Paris we arrived with 20 minutes to kick-off. My recall is that I did not referee particularly well, matters not helped by a glue-like pitch. While the French were fascinated that I could chat away with them, by the end of play any positive assessment was more for linguistic ability than for my performance.

Having survived my first year back 'in Europe', it was to be more of the same the following season.

Firstly, I was off to Stradey Park in Wales, home of

The Ref's Call

Llanelli, for their local derby match against near neighbours Neath. The two towns are less than 20 kilometres apart, and their rugby rivalry has always been on the upper scale of intense. I had strolled around that morning and witnessed the severe effects of a broken economy. Few people were in town, and those that had things to do were scurrying in and out of small, fairly run-down shops. Later on, as I walked from the hotel, I was amazed to see the hordes of supporters of both teams heading to the ground; it was packed, a complete sell-out. Even in hard times, the Welsh love their rugby and, for Saturday afternoons at least, everything else could be forgotten.

This fixture – a match that we can say euphemistically was 'hard-fought' – came with a high degree of difficulty from a refereeing standpoint. Equipped with only two touch judges, one supplied by each team, even informal assistance was unlikely to be forthcoming. The two packs went at it hammer and tongs; there was an atmosphere of high tension. Whatever growing reputation I was earning for letting play flow looked like it might now be in jeopardy.

After about 15 minutes, the scores were even, but all from penalty kicks for foul play. At yet another break in play, Llanelli captain Ray Gravell approached me. I was expecting the worst but rather than criticism, the legendary Wales and Lions centre had simple words of encouragement that convinced me I was doing the right thing, Sticking to my guns, the message got to the players and before long, it was a good game of rugby rather than a fight that broke out.

Some time afterwards, when I spoke to Welsh referee Derek Bevan about my experience at Stradey Park, he laughingly told me that I had only been given that match because no referee in Wales wanted to do it, adding, 'There's always a bad outbreak of referee influenza when that one comes around.'

The next lesson I learned was that while you're only as good as your last match, you're also only as good as your next one. A week after Llanelli, I was in Aberdeen at the Gordonians club, where the home team were due to welcome Gala from the Borders. For this match, my normally assiduous preparation consisted of little more than a quick look at the Scottish league table during the week. It showed that Gala were comfortably in first position, while the hosts were, equally comfortably, at the bottom. Only one outcome here, I was thinking, as the train travelled north from Edinburgh along the most scenic of coastlines.

When I arrived at the ground a few hours before kick-off, I was surprised to see a very substantial crowd already settling into the stands, and that the television cameras were setting up. Unbeknownst to me, Gordonians waited eagerly for this annual visit from Gala, always more than determined to punch above their weight when these particular opponents came to town. For the first half an hour of the match, the pitch resembled something from the battlefield scenes in *Braveheart*. Unlike the recent debacle at Llanelli, I was not ready for anything like this – but then Ray Gravell's rallying words echoed from somewhere in my brain, and I really went hard at it and successfully pulled the teams back into line.

The natural next step in my career on the rugby pitch was a big one – being entrusted with international Test matches. While others might have been daunted at the prospect, I was champing at the bit.

In my day, after a few years of being tested in Europe, moving through matches across the four other unions, a referee was either seen as eligible for the final step, or excluded from ever making it. Eligibility didn't necessarily mean success, it also depended a lot on timing.

Each union was entitled to select three referees, on an annual basis, for its international panel; although for a few seasons it curiously went, unnecessarily, to five. If this panel was fairly young and going well, it was unlikely that a union would make room for a new boy and select him instead. Also, if there were two or three guys becoming eligible, but only one place available, then some would inevitably lose out.

The final step was out of my hands. There wasn't much more to do now but wait.

Chapter Six

20 May 1984

*Romania v Scotland in Bucharest
(International Test match on Scotland tour)*

As we were driven from the airport in two black limos, a large group of sullen-faced teenage girls immediately started to jump about and cheer, all waving a Romanian flag.

But when they realised that we were not their leader, whose flight had landed around the same time as ours, the flags dropped and the sad expressions returned.

That evening, if any Romanian turned on their state-run, propaganda-fuelled, only TV station, all they would have seen was Nicolae Ceauşescu being greeted with

*wild enthusiasm and flag-waving; it was shown
continuously.*

They were the only smiles we saw all trip.

• • •

By the time December 1983 rolled around, I was still
waiting. I'd had a taste of the international game as far back
as 1978 when Ireland played Scotland at Lansdowne Road,
but on the touchline rather than as the man in the middle.
It may be hard to believe that, in those days, it was the
prerogative of the IRFU president to select the 'Irish' touch
judge, and the incumbent, Jack Coffey of the Lansdowne
club, had given me the nod.

The match was refereed by Englishman Peter Hughes,
accompanied by fellow countryman Alan Welsby, who was
the substitute referee and the other touch judge. A lot of the
time before kick-off was spent looking at the sky, considering
the weather, and wondering whether the touch judges should
wear blazers or tracksuits. For the record, Ireland won 12–9,
and for the fashionistas, the touch judges wore tracksuits.

I had been extremely grateful for the opportunity but it
only whetted my appetite for the main job, and almost six
years on, that hunger had yet to be sated. I had now spent

the previous few seasons doing the rounds of the other unions, refereeing their top matches. You could not afford to have a poor performance, including matches in Ireland, particularly the interprovincials.

Over my career, there were several Irish referees who missed the boat narrowly. Denis Templeton from Belfast was one who came very close, but was ultimately denied. Dubliner Des Lamont from Terenure RFC was on the verge too, but his chances disappeared in desperately unfortunate fashion.

He was refereeing the first floodlit match at Lansdowne Road, an All Ireland League (AIL) game between the two resident clubs, Lansdowne and Wanderers, when his Achilles tendon snapped. Apart from that particular injury being exceptionally painful, rather like being stabbed suddenly with a very sharp knife, it is career-threatening. When Lamont was told that it would mean months in plaster to have any chance of a full repair, he knew his days with the whistle were over.

Could both these men have refereed in the Five Nations in different circumstances? Without a shadow of a doubt. Luck, good or bad, always plays a part.

Ahead of the 1984 international season, I felt I had a realistic chance, even though the inscrutable advisory committee kept their cards notoriously close to their chests. In fact, the week before the announcement, I had travelled back from Belfast with one of them, former Test referee Kevin Kelleher, who had just watched me referee in Malone

The Ref's Call

RFC. The selection was due to be announced the following Monday.

Would he give me a hint? Would he what. As we got off the train in Dublin, all he said was, 'Let me put you out of your misery . . . we've postponed our decision for a week.' So, deep in misery I remained.

A week later, still no call as I prowled around, staring at the silent phone. Well, I thought, it won't ring if I'm not selected, so I checked in with Dave Burnett who was a racing certainty to retain his place; no, he'd heard nothing, leaving me with some hope to hold on to.

Finally, the phone did ring. I snatched up the handset to hear the voice of Bob Fitzgerald, who was then Secretary-Treasurer of the IRFU. He spoke briefly. 'The international panel for the coming season is David Burnett, Owen Doyle and John West.' I had made it, by heck, and it felt wonderful.

That said, I knew that even if selected, the Five Nations committee would designate internationals to each union, who would then appoint one of their panel to those matches. There were usually only two matches per country, so even this selection didn't mean there was a guarantee of a Five Nations match.

But Fitzgerald hadn't finished. 'The appointments are as follows: 21 January, Wales v Scotland in Cardiff, referee Owen Doyle . . .' The rest was a blur. I can honestly say that boggled me; I had not expected a Five Nations match so soon, thinking that a game as touch judge and an autumn international with the whistle were more likely. And suddenly I wasn't sure I wanted it. It would be very much a case of in at the deep end. Christmas would be frugal and fasting.

And so, on 20 January 1984, the three of us set off for Cardiff. I had been greatly encouraged by the many letters I had received from clubs all over the country, congratulating me and wishing me well. Even from clubs who had, with justification, been 'frustrated' with some of my decisions from time to time.

We arrived at the Angel Hotel just as dusk was falling. I walked down to Cardiff Arms Park and, finding a side gate open, was able to slip into the famous stadium and stand in the middle of the pitch. It was awesome even when empty, and spine-tingling to imagine that the next day this vast arena would be packed to the rafters. And I'd be standing in the middle. It was easy to wonder why Burnett or West wouldn't be refereeing, and they may well have been thinking the same thing.

Just then, a tannoy pinged in, and a hollow voice echoed around the ground: 'Get off the damn pitch, don't you know there's a match here tomorrow.' The man behind that voice was the very likeable groundsman Bill Hardiman, who quickly escorted me back through the gate.

The limbic part of our brain holds the key to our very basic primitive emotions – fight, flight or freeze. In his fascinating book *The Chimp Paradox*, leading psychiatrist Steve Peters has described it as our inner chimp.

The next morning my own chimp was having a real go

– as in screaming 'get out of here' – as I watched busloads of kilt-wearing Scots descending on the pubs. So a long walk seemed like a good idea; it was about 11 a.m., and I put my watch in my pocket. Having walked through a nearby park for what I thought was the guts of an hour, it seemed time for a light lunch. But when I looked at my watch it was only 11.20. Time, and the chimp, were playing their tricks.

After checking my kit for the umpteenth time, at one o'clock we got ready to walk from the hotel to the ground, which is situated right in the city centre. The bars and the foyer were jammed, as we made our way downstairs and through the throngs both inside and outside the hotel. Advice was freely given, some very witty, some inevitably a little on the hostile side, but nothing remotely threatening. It was a rite of passage, a sort of coming-of-age moment.

As ever, pre-match, the referee was responsible for checking the studs of the players and I knocked on the Welsh dressing-room door to do so. I was asked to wait outside for just a moment, and the door closed again. Several seconds later – though it seemed like an age – the door was reopened, and I was handed a bucket full of studs. I looked blankly at the bucket and back into the dressing room, when suddenly there were grins all round – it was, apparently, a way of making a new boy on the block feel welcome.

In contrast to my morning walk, the game swept by in a

blur, players choosing options and moving the ball at high speed. In that era, both the referee and the assistants kept the time, and I was shocked when Dave Burnett said, 'Three minutes to half-time.' It seemed to me like we'd only started, but time was playing its tricks again.

Early on, Wales set out to unnerve the Scots and tested me with some very aggressive play. There were no cards back then, and players had to believe that the ultimate sanction would come if necessary. 'Stern words' were needed. In fact, Wales' John Perkins got a very clear warning at an early lineout for a wild swinging punch. It was lucky for both him and his opponent that he didn't connect.

The teams were evenly matched, particularly up front, but Scotland had the edge at half-back, where the Roy Laidlaw–John Rutherford pairing managed possession in way that would still be admired and have a place in today's game. Their instinctive feel for the right time to kick, and the right time for Rutherford to run it, was unparalleled.

The packs pretty much held equal sway, with Wales fielding players such as 'Staff' Jones, Bob Norster and Dick Moriarty, and captained by the ever affable Eddie Butler, who would later become a BBC rugby commentator. Another future notable was Dai Pickering at number seven, who would go on to become a very influential figure in Welsh Rugby Union (WRU) and World Rugby circles.

The Scotland pack included Colin Deans, Iain Milne, Jim Calder and David Leslie, and they did not give one inch in the Cardiff cauldron.

The Ref's Call

Captained from prop by Jim Aitken, the Scots scored two tries (one apiece for Aitken and Iain Paxton), with Wales' Mark Titley the only man to cross for the home side. The final score of 15–9 turned out to be the first leg of a Scottish Grand Slam-winning season.

It was also the start of a very bad run for Wales with me as referee; I reffed them about six times and they never won. While they weren't going through a very strong spell, struggling to emerge from the shadow of the great Welsh teams of the 1970s, it's a strange statistic nonetheless.

That things didn't bode well for them when I was around was underlined nearly 10 years later when Canada's Gareth Rees split the posts with a last-minute touchline conversion in Cardiff. It was a nigh-on impossible kick into a strong gale as the rain pelted down, and gave Canada their greatest moment in a totally unexpected 26–24 win. The underdogs had barely passed the ball all match in the awful conditions and the try-scoring move took Wales totally by surprise.

I saw more of that Scotland squad a few months later, albeit in more unusual circumstances, after being selected alongside Michael Rea and Dave Burnett to officiate on their three-match tour of Romania, then still under the iron grip of communist dictator Nicolae Ceaușescu. The trip would culminate in a Test match against the national team, with me in the middle.

We landed in Bucharest to find an airport jam-packed with soldiers who were armed to the teeth, snipers on rooftops, soldiers with machine guns surrounding the tarmac, and an armoured car to top things off. While it seemed overkill for our arrival, it turned out that Ceaușescu's private plane was due to land at any moment.

After much wrangling at passport control, and the pawning off of many IRFU shamrock pins, we were allowed through, to be greeted by what we thought were Romanian rugby officials but who turned out to be members of the Securitate, or secret police, who 'minded' us for the entire trip.

The use of rugby as a propaganda weapon was certainly an eye-opener. Ceaușescu seconded players from the army who played for Steaua Bucharest and also from the police, whose team was Dinamo Bucharest. This ensured that the Romanian national side were perfectly capable of beating those capitalist nations in the west, with some notable results against Five Nations sides during that era. They had toured Ireland in 1980, beating three of the provinces, with only Leinster managing a victory, before a 13–13 draw against an Irish XV in a non-Test match.

We were brought out to dinner most evenings in the company of our two 'bodyguards'. After we'd returned to one of our rooms one night, while having our compulsory nightcap, we had a moan to ourselves about the cuisine. Except it wasn't just to ourselves. The next day, our driver said that he believed we didn't like Romanian food and this prompted a tour of the hotel's basement where we came across two headset-wearing, plain-clothes Securitate, listening into conversations as large wheels of tape were turning on the recording machine.

The Ref's Call

Occasionally, we got time to ourselves to walk in the local park, where, inevitably, we would be stealthily approached by a local offering to exchange amounts of the useless currency, the leu, for sterling or dollars. This regime had created a crestfallen society that had no hope of a better future. Despite this, the Romanian rugby people were very friendly and extended as much hospitality as their limited means allowed. We could not complain.

The game against Scotland was played on a scorching May afternoon, the temperature at what felt just below boiling point. Some 20,000 turned up but were lost in the vast stadium. The crowd included 31 Scottish supporters, among them the future mayor of Haslemere, Brian Howard MBE. They were a great group, and it has been my pleasure to have remained in touch with Brian ever since. It might remain the only time when supporters were invited to attend the post-match banquet, even if they had to cough up a few pounds to do so.

It was a defeat for the Grand Slam winners, 28–22 – deserved by Romania, and certainly no shame for Scotland. We went to sleep at about two in the morning, Scottish bagpipes still sounding out over the city.

As a footnote to history, Ceauşescu and his wife Elena were captured and executed on Christmas Day 1989, during the revolution which also very sadly claimed the life of the outstanding wing-forward and captain Florică Murariu. He had led his country to that victory just five years earlier.

I was back at the Arms Park the following November for the Test between Wales and Australia. My 'assistants' were again Dave Burnett and John West. It's funny how the brain adjusts and, this time, I was much more relaxed about things. While the noise from the crowd was exactly the same as it had been for the Scotland match, it was no longer invasive, so my inner chimp remained at rest. Very happily, he stayed like that for the rest of my career and I always felt I had the right balance of adrenalin and composure. Both are needed.

Another thing that was different was how loud the pre-match singing sounded in our dressing room. Normally, from the bowels of the stadium, you could only hear it in the distance. Curious as to the reason, we looked into the small pathway behind the changing rooms and our 'investigations' showed that Wales had placed loudspeakers there, pointing at the Australia changing rooms in an effort to intimidate the visitors.

Australia were quite pleased to see me, as the previous year I'd reffed the guts of their team in Grenoble against a France Selected XV. The evening before that match, I'd met Wallaby captain Andy Slack at the local mayor's reception for the teams and officials. I'd known him since his time playing for the Wanderers club in Dublin. He said it was a very physical tour and that I could expect a rough one. Australia would not be holding back.

I asked him if they could keep it cool for 15 minutes if things needed to be sorted out, to cut me a little slack, as it were, and he agreed. To French amazement, their early overaggresssive rucking was met with unexpected Australian passivity – the Aussies actually stepped back – and that made it very easy for me to make my mark.

It turned out to be an excellent Wallaby performance; running the ball from everywhere, they won easily, 27–7, in a game that was simple to let flow. The French press heaped a lot of praise on me the next day. Accept it when you get it, as it doesn't come too often. What they never knew about, of course, was the meeting the evening before the match that had helped smooth the path.

Now in Cardiff, and captained again by Slack, this was one of the best Aussie teams to visit the northern hemisphere, and they 'Grand-Slammed' their way through that autumn '84 tour. In a total of 18 matches, they did lose four midweek games, including to Cardiff (with the debonair Belfast man Denis Templeton in charge) and to Ulster. But they won all of their Tests, and by the time of the Welsh match, England and Ireland had already been beaten.

They were, by this point, a very well-oiled machine. Bristling with talent both 'fore and aft', the backs were full of silky runners – Nick Farr-Jones, Mark Ella, Michael Lynagh and David Campese. The towering Roger Gould was at full-back; to this day, I'm not sure if I've ever seen anyone boot a ball farther.

Up front, the pack included the two massive Steves, Cutler and Williams, at lock was Simon Poidevin with Steve

Tuynman in the back row, and the awesome front row of Topo Rodriguez, Tom Lawton and Andy McIntyre.

Even the very experienced Welsh pack (including Perkins, Norster, Davies and Butler) could not withstand an almighty five-metre scrum, and were shunted over their line for a Wallaby pushover try.

It was the complete team, coached superbly by the indefatigable Alan Jones. He would later become a top media performer in Australia, hosting various radio talk shows. Unsurprisingly, he has always been forthright in his opinions.

Completely immersed with getting every dot and comma right, Jones knocked on my hotel door the evening before the match to 'have that chat' we promised each other. Well, we hadn't, so I didn't but, armed with flip chart and pens, he outlined two planned moves for the next day.

It turned out to be a really helpful meeting as one move was clearly illegal, and so it remained unused on the day. If it had been utilised, I wonder if I would have picked it up in the heat of battle – to be honest, I'm not so sure. That sort of encounter was really the precursor to the more formally planned meetings between coaches and referees that are an inherent part of the game today.

The match itself was a classic. The first Australian try came from a well-rehearsed move following a lineout and, thanks to my meeting with Jones, I knew what was coming. A terrific break by David Campese saw Simon Poidevin take an inside pass and offload to send Michael Lynagh shooting in under the posts. Wales resisted well and never gave up, with David Bishop scoring the only try Australia conceded in their four Test matches. Late scores, including a Mark Ella intercept try, pushed the final score out to 28–9.

It was the early days of touch judges 'flagging', and the system required them to raise their flag horizontally and point it towards the goal line of a team guilty of foul play. Australia were pressing very hard, about five metres from the Welsh line, when John West flagged for foul play and then told me, correctly, that Wales were the offenders. We were both aghast to realise that West had, completely inadvertently, flagged the wrong way. When I explained matters to a very disgruntled Welsh captain, hooker Mike Watkins, that the subsequent penalty had to, and did, go to Australia, the roof nearly came off the stands such was the roar of disapproval from the crowd. It was reported that structural engineers were called in the next day to check the condition of that roof.

But the crowd, and indeed the speakers that had near-deafened us pre-match, were unsurprisingly silent as the hosts trooped back in after their beating.

Burnett and myself returned to Dublin the next morning in high winds, the antics of the turbo-propeller plane making for a white-knuckle ride home. West, a teacher by profession, was annoyingly so undisturbed by these high-flying events that he was actually correcting maths papers as we were buffeted across the Irish Sea.

Every international was an enjoyable privilege to

officiate, either as referee or assistant. The days before it all became professional, we were very well 'expensed' and stayed in the best of hotels. The five-star Grand Hotel, near the Opéra in Paris, was a very definite favourite. It was a wonderful way to see the world, experiencing different cultures and cuisines along the way.

A match I found hard to enjoy, although it had nothing to do with my own performance, was Newport v New Zealand in 1989. Newport had famously been the only team to beat Wilson Whineray's 1963–64 touring All Blacks, thanks to a solitary drop kick by centre Dick Uzzell. But by the time Wayne 'Buck' Shelford and his men arrived in town 25 years later, Newport were in disarray. The referee assistants for the day were Stephen Hilditch and Philip Grey.

In another strange coincidence, Gwynne Walters, who I had first met as a child in Dartry, had refereed the 1963 match.

Newport had been having a poor season and had no choice but to field a young team, having recently lost some very good players to other clubs. Jon Callard, for example, had left for Bath, where he joined current Sky commentator and rugby writer Stuart Barnes, also previously of Newport. Both would win many caps with England.

Coached by Alex Wylie, these All Blacks were as uncompromising a team as you could ever come across. Wylie would much later on take up a coaching role with Clontarf RFC in Dublin. The All Blacks won all their matches on that tour of Wales and Ireland, but I'm not sure if they made many friends along the way. They were a dour lot but results are results, and history shows that Shelford never lost a match as captain, a draw against Australia his only blemish. Quite some record, albeit over a shortish, three-year stint.

On this particular occasion, Newport had decided to huddle in their 22 for the haka, but Shelford led his team down to them and performed it there. A few days later, in Dublin, Willie Anderson would famously take a different approach, as he advanced the Irish team towards the haka, the Ireland players linking arms and eyeballing the opposition. The teams got perilously close and for a hair-raising moment it looked as if hostilities would break out before kick-off.

The weather was perfect in Newport but, from the start, New Zealand were intent on high levels of intimidation, and typically ferocious rucking. Of course, intimidation is part of the game, but it seemed to be just too much; it was really a case of men against boys, and one could sense the result from very early on. They had also picked a team that left nothing to chance – both Shelford and Zinzan Brooke were in the back row, Grant Fox and Graeme Bachop the half-backs, with John Gallagher at full-back.

The pressure on the Newport scrum was immense, and they couldn't cope with either the weight or technique of the opposition. It was potentially dangerous, so I asked

New Zealand to ease off their shove at scrum time, a very unusual step to take at this level. Understandably, this request did not go down well.

However, this unpopular stance did get some response, but, despite it, at least one of Newport's front row was forced off with a shoulder injury. As a by-the-way, it was also my first meeting with future Ireland, Wales and Lions coach Warren Gatland, who lined out at hooker.

Later in the match, there was a punch, delivered by an All Black, which removed several front teeth of Andrew Pocock, the young Newport back-row. Captain Shelford seemed to have had his jersey tugged, maybe more, maybe he received a punch, but the NZ retaliation was very swift and very hard. As officials, we were pretty sure who the culprit was, without being 100 per cent certain. How we could have done with a TMO – everything would have been sorted on the spot.

Suspecting it was Shelford, I asked him why he had hit the Newport player, a question worthy, I thought, of a senior counsel. I'd hoped it would have got a response along the lines that he, Shelford, had been hit first. But no, he was well ahead of me, and said that it had not been him. From his point of view, it was a great answer. Rightly or wrongly, that sowed enough doubt in my mind that thoughts of sending him off quickly receded. The other side of the coin here is that if you interfere with a New Zealander going for the ball, well, you're not going to get away with it lightly.

The Ref's Call

After the match, the finger of blame was pointing in one direction only, and it was disappointing not to have dealt with it fully on the pitch. In today's money, it would probably have been one yellow card for Newport and one red for New Zealand. As things were, however, all I could do was issue a very clear and final warning.

Shelford had famously also escaped a sending-off two years earlier in the World Cup semi-final. Huw Richards of Wales threw a punch; it was spotted by Shelford, who responded with a right hook that would have done credit to Muhammad Ali. Richards was knocked out cold and, when he was revived, was sent off by referee Kerry Fitzgerald. How Shelford remained on the pitch, and did not suffer a similar fate, is a mystery, and he would go on to make a major contribution to New Zealand's win in the final against Australia.

In many ways, the attitude of the All Blacks that day in Newport would have been understandable if it had been a close, tough and equal contest. But in a match they won 54–9, and by 10 tries to one? It has always seemed to me that they could have got the same score in a less overtly aggressive way, and thereby shown their opponents a little more respect.

The counterargument is, of course, that playing the way they did is an indelible and unchangeable part of their DNA. They would also have been fully aware of history, and it would have been important to avenge that defeat Newport inflicted on Wilson Whineray's All Blacks in

1963. History was not to be allowed repeat itself. They had come to do a job and, my word, they did it.

Newport had arranged a splendid dinner to welcome their distinguished visitors, but the formalities went on too long for the All Blacks. They made an early speech of thanks, and then all trooped out quite some time before the evening was over, which was a shame.

When, in 1990, it was decided that Shelford was surplus to requirements, there was a huge outburst of public disagreement. A sustained 'Bring back Buck' campaign was launched, but to no avail. Nonetheless, Wayne 'Buck' Shelford has not been forgotten. In 2021, he was honoured with a knighthood in Queen Elizabeth's birthday honours list.

Chapter Seven

16 January 1988

France v England in Paris
(First match of that year's Five Nations)

France were holding on as England set up another attack. They broke up the left touchline and, suddenly, centre Kevin Simms was free and heading for the corner – it seemed nothing was going to stop him.

I headed for the same place, and was far too close to him when he decided that he might not make it after all. The inside pass he threw was directed towards the swarming England support – except that's where I was also to be found, and the pass went to me.

The French defenders were all over the place, including all over me, and the potential try-scoring opportunity was lost. It *was, by a country mile, my worst international moment. 'Le Crunch' indeed.*

. . .

Given the time I spent living and working in France during my youth, refereeing over there was always special for me. And while it was generally very difficult to control, the annual battle between England and France, colloquially known as 'Le Crunch', was a huge fixture to be a part of. It has always been, and will always be, one of the most keenly anticipated Five/Six Nations matches.

Former French international centre Jean-Pierre Lux, speaking at a dinner in London, once famously joked that although he really liked the English, sometimes they made it really hard for him to do so: 'This afternoon they collected me at Waterloo Station, and this evening I have just been served a dish of Beef Wellington.'

Perhaps it does date back to Napoleon's defeat on that bloody Belgian field outside Waterloo; maybe it was Winston Churchill, who was distinctly unamused by the defeatism of Frenchman Marshal Philippe Pétain. In 1940, Churchill chose 21 October for his address to the French nation – the anniversary of Trafalgar Day when Horatio Nelson routed the French, and the Spanish for good measure.

These two countries have been at it for quite a while now.

The Ref's Call

However, in the late 1980s and early '90s 'Le Crunch' reached unacceptable levels of violence and intimidation. France had been dominant during the 1980s, reaching the 1987 Rugby World Cup final, and had beaten England in four successive Five Nations matches. England were determined to turn this around, and their 1989 victory at Twickenham was the first of eight wins in a row.

Those matches brought myself, and fellow Irishmen Stephen Hilditch and Brian Stirling, to Parc des Princes and Twickenham on no less than five occasions. Given the history between the sides, let alone the nations, these were notoriously difficult challenges and we definitely could have done with the presence of a TMO, if only for reasons of self-preservation.

A visit to Paris in 1985 saw Hilditch and myself travel in the role of touch judges for visiting South African Steve Strydom, who had come to referee the France v Wales Five Nations fixture.

The French had organised a large dinner party for the Friday evening, and we travelled some distance out of Paris to the very unusual setting of a supermarket. The normal canteen had been transformed into a very posh seafood restaurant; the array of oysters, prawns, lobsters and other shellfish was stunning. The only problem was: how could the match officials for the following day risk a bad oyster or indeed any sort of food poisoning, unlikely as it was. So we nibbled on bread and had a couple of glasses of wine, but when the cheese and absolutely mouth-watering desserts arrived, things suddenly took a turn for the better. However, before we could get stuck in, Strydom became worried about the time. It was indeed getting late and, understandably, he wanted to get us back to the hotel, which we duly did, missing out altogether on the wonderful platters which had just been wheeled in.

On the morning of the match, word came in that there were some threats to Strydom on account of planned demonstrations about the yet-to-be-resolved issues of apartheid. The French Federation was concerned that if anything untoward should happen to him, another referee would be needed, so it was decided that we would not all journey together to Parc des Princes. I managed to get into the wrong car, and was shocked when Strydom hopped in after me. We travelled at high speed, even more so than the usual match-day trip to a ground. It was an uncomfortable journey; I thought that if the protesters don't get us, this driver will do the job for them. As it happened, we arrived safely, without as much as a sign of protest.

The two France v England matches I took charge of were in 1988 and 1990. Both were played in Parc des Princes, a venue I really liked, even though it only held about 50,000 spectators. The construction was of reinforced concrete, and the sound of the French brass bands reverberated and echoed strongly around the ground. It was a mad noise and the atmosphere was always hot. Its location, in the 16th arrondissement of Paris, gave matches a great city feel to them. In contrast, the Stade de France, a wonderful stadium which holds over 80,000 and is situated outside the city, is a much more impersonal place.

Both of these matches were tough, and presented stiff challenges for the match officials. England lost the 1988 match very narrowly, 9–10, and I was held largely responsible. They had started very well, and should have had two early tries; one looked a clear certainty but they managed to butcher the clearest of overlaps deep inside the French 22, deciding instead to try and plough through the last defenders, which failed miserably. The backs, including Will Carling and Rory Underwood, were less than thrilled.

Their mood wasn't helped when my untimely interception butchered their second opportunity. That was as close as they would come to crossing, their nine-point haul coming from two Jonathan Webb penalties and a Les Cusworth drop goal. I didn't have too many bad moments, but that was high on the Richter scale.

The reason for that error? Well, I was known more for a certain casualness of movement than great pace about the place, but I compensated with anticipation and positioning. Unfortunately, that day was over-anticipation of the highest order, and my attempt to get there before the action went badly askew for once. The result was that I'd put myself in the worst spot I could possibly have chosen, a severe case of being in the wrong place at the wrong time.

That moment invented the term 'player space' for me

and it's the area where a referee, in any sport, should never find him or herself. The danger of this was highlighted by what happened to French referee Mathieu Raynal during the 2012–13 season. Montpellier were at home to Racing in the French Top 14 league when, midway through the second half, he got badly caught between two players. He suffered a horrific double fracture of his tibia and fibula and, for good measure, also fractured his collar bone.

While I had suffered damage to no more than my pride, Raynal had been in the equivalent of a car crash. With great determination, and no little nerve, he returned to refereeing after just one year out.

My second France v England match was two years later, and it was altogether a happier day at the office, with England running out easy winners, 26–7.

That match was notable for an unusual delayed start. As the teams left the dressing rooms and prepared to take the field, we discovered that the sliding glass doors that opened onto the pitch remained firmly shut. It turned out that France's President François Mitterrand had not yet finished his cognac and coffee. Quite obviously, it was impossible for the teams to go out before the great man was ready.

So the two teams were lined up together and, with nowhere to go, they decided it was perfectly natural to start some minor hostilities while they were waiting. Don't forget, players are 'up to 90' at this point, full of high-octane adrenalin. As I asked for calm, and that hostilities should at least cease until the match started, the opening bars of *La Marseillaise* rang out and those doors slid open. Mitterrand was, at last, taking his seat.

These 'crunches' could often begin with quite a bang, and, in one of those matches, I had exactly that sort of start. French scrum-half Pierre Berbizier fielded an early kick and, with nowhere positive to go, decided to step into touch. The ubiquitous Mickey Skinner decided to help him on his way and hard-shouldered him over the line. In a flash, Skinner was himself 'taken out' by French prop Jean-Pierre Garuet, who had taken grave exception to the hit on Berbizier. In truth, these early flashpoints can be real opportunities for a referee. If handled correctly, the sting can be taken out of the match very early on, and the underlying current of tension can disappear rather than simmer just below boiling point for a long time.

Quietly but firmly, they were told that this had to be the end, and that any more from them would have just one result. Fortunately, the message was not only transmitted but, unlike on some occasions, also received by players who knew they were in the last-chance saloon. Some years later, when I met him at a European Cup match, Garuet thanked me for not sending him off that day – he had been dismissed by Welsh referee Clive Norling against Ireland during his first Five Nations in 1984. To be sent off again just as his career wound down would, he said with a wide smile, have been a controversy too far.

Those days were also the early days of drug-testing, with

a player's number from each team being drawn from a bowl before kick-off. After the match, it was a very unwelcome and additional role for the assistant referees to go to the dressing rooms and extract the relevant players.

France lost to England at Twickenham in 1989 with Stephen Hilditch refereeing, so the intrepid Stirling and I headed off to do our duty. Now, the losing dressing room is not a place any match official wants to be, so we knocked on the door and, after gaining entry, simply said that we needed number 16 for the test, *merci*. And there he was swapping his jersey with a team-mate who now 'became' number 16. Well, all we were told to do was get the number 16, which we did, deciding discretion was a lot better than valour, which would have meant insisting that they swap back the jerseys again.

It's impossible, when thinking of these matches, not to reference the rumours that later came out about the use of amphetamines in French sides during this period. 1986's infamous Second Test between France and New Zealand became known as the 'Battle of Nantes', due to the levels of violence in the match. I'm sure there wasn't a banned substance list at that point, so those rumours may well not have been so far from the truth; the then French team doctor Jacques Mombet alleged their use in Pierre Ballester's 2015 book *Rugby à Charges: L'enquête Choc* (*The Case Against Rugby*).

The aforementioned 'Buck' Shelford was to the fore in that battle, eventually being laid out and losing some teeth, as New Zealand won 16–3. Earlier in the match, he had left the field for some stitches; nothing particularly unusual, except that these were to mend a very nasty tear to his scrotum. When everything had been neatly put back in place he returned to the fray, the teak-toughest of men.

There was disturbing, shocking and very sad news some 10 years later. French forward Marc Cécillon, who featured in several of those 'Le Crunch' matches, had played on until 1995, when he retired. Immensely strong, he had always played without fuss; he just got on with his job and very effectively too, his demeanour earning him the nickname 'The Quiet Man'.

Not so off the pitch – always fond of very much more than a quiet drink, he could not adapt to retirement. His drinking became very serious and, coupled with bouts of depression, was a severe problem for him and his family. In 2004, after an argument with his wife Chantal at a barbecue in a neighbouring village, he left the party to go home. At some point, he snapped and, returning armed with a revolver, shot her dead in front of 60 guests. He apparently didn't know what he had done until told by the *gendarmerie* the next morning. He served seven years of a 14-year sentence.

There is no doubt whatsoever that an ability to converse in the language of both teams is a huge bonus. My mother's French heritage was clear from her maiden name, Pélissier, but I had decided to keep that quiet, having been all too aware of the difficulties a certain Irish referee, David Ingram Henderson Burnett, in his attempts to prove that he wasn't Scottish. But the linguistic ability I had picked up on those sojourns to France meant fortune was with me in that regard when it came to 'Le Crunch'.

In fact, before the 1990 fixture, English captain Will Carling asked me if I wouldn't mind repeating in English anything I said in French. Not being able to communicate with one of the teams in moments of high tension undoubtedly makes the task more difficult. However, no amount of French-speaking could have prevented the events that unfolded in February 1992 in Paris when Stephen Hilditch was the man in the middle, with myself and Brian Stirling his assistants. In fact, had Hilditch been the Master of the Tower of Babel, it would have been to no avail.

The sides had played a torrid encounter at Parc des Princes the previous October in a World Cup quarter-final. The English had torn into the French from the off, and France had felt that their aggression was way over the top, though they themselves were no shrinking violets. That match was refereed by New Zealander David Bishop, a fine referee, with Hilditch and Bishop's fellow countryman Keith Lawrence on the touchlines. I was the designated fourth official, which had its own amusing little story. Nobody had considered where I should sit, so a French official put me in the front row of the stand, in a premium seat – or, rather, two premium seats.

Before kick-off, two Frenchmen claimed these seats with

what looked like perfectly valid tickets, but I played dumb and wouldn't move. When they returned with two armed *gendarmes* plus a German shepherd, I was, of course, more than happy to vacate, and with quite some alacrity. I watched the match on a pitchside chair, an even better view as it turned out.

Before the match, Bishop had visited both teams to discuss, in particular, front-row issues, and what he would expect from them at 'scrum time'. I translated for him in the French dressing room. In response to his comments on the scrum, France coach and the man who had been captain for the 'battle of Nantes', Daniel Dubroca, looked at me and said, 'Ask him what he's going to do about the lineouts.' To which Bishop's response was, 'Let's take them as they come.'

Dubroca just shrugged, growling, 'Then tell him we'll take the scrums as they come too, have a good day.' But there was little chance of that – or, more accurately, no chance at all.

From the get-go there was mayhem, as England piled on huge pressure. High balls were launched deep into the French 22, and Serge Blanco, while fielding these well, was the target of the English follow-up. On the first occasion he was tackled he lost possession, and then was needlessly 'shoed' in the ruck that followed. The next high ball, he made a mark and was hit late by Nigel Heslop, who may or may not have heard the whistle. Blanco had had enough and swung a punch at Heslop, who was then laid out by

Éric Champ. A very interesting sequence of events, particularly for a World Cup quarter-final.

Later, as the tension continued, Rob Andrew, having held back Philippe Sella, also needed treatment following Sella's 'retaliatory punch'. It was grim stuff.

Somewhat by the way, the result: England scored a late converted try from a maul drive to seal a 19–10 win. Carling, unusually finding himself in the maul, managed to rip the ball from a surprised French player for the vital insurance score. Largely forgotten amid the madness was a truly superb English try by Rory Underwood, the recipient of a wonder pass from Jeremy Guscott, after the latter had scythed through the defence.

Nothing, though, was ever going to convince the French that they hadn't had a rough ride from the referee. After the match, as we made our way back to the dressing rooms, Dubroca 'approached' David Bishop, manhandling him as he vented his spleen in no uncertain fashion. I wasn't close enough to hear the actual words, but – later on – the word 'cheat' was in the air. Or should I say 'on the air'.

It was the very early days of officials being 'miked-up', but their communication was only allowed to go to the commentators and to the press; at that point, the crowd or TV audience were not yet privy to these conversations. But Dubroca's words were heard by well over a hundred eager journalistic ears.

The coach was left with no choice but to resign and was replaced by former French scrum-half Pierre Berbizier just a year after he had retired from playing. Despite this speedy entry to international coaching, Berbizier would lead France to the World Cup semi-finals in 1995.

When the Five Nations came around a mere six months after that World Cup meeting, there was no doubt that France were not going to be intimidated in Paris, and that neither team would give an inch. The pre-match atmosphere was tense but, given what we had seen in October, no more than we were anticipating. Or so we thought.

Being frank, nothing could have prepared us for the events of the second half. The last 20 minutes were particularly awful, and nothing to do with rugby. Every ounce of our cumulative experience was needed to keep a modicum of control in what was a shameful second half.

It was the first, and only, time that two players from one team were sent off in Five Nations history, the French front-rowers Vincent Moscato and Grégoire Lascube both dismissed.

Although they had not started well, and France scored the first try, England led 15–4 at half-time. This included a penalty try from a five-metre scrum, an absolutely correct decision but which did not, of course, go down well with the French – the team were fired up, and so was the crowd. When, later on, a lineout penalty decision went against them as they broke away towards the English 22, the team and all of France decided that the whole world was out to get them.

Hilditch, Stirling and myself took the brunt of the crowd's

anger; it was nasty, very hostile and very far indeed from the usual crowd reaction to unpopular decisions.

As England tightened their grip on the match, the French discipline began to plummet, not helped by the fact that their captain Philippe Sella had gone off injured. I'm not sure who took over the captaincy but the French team were rudderless at that point.

First, Lascube stamped on – now rugby pundit – Martin Bayfield's head, an incident that I managed to see. I instantly flagged it to Stephen, and kept my eyes glued to the player to be certain I could identify him correctly. Several English players were turning towards Lascube for retribution, but were stopped by an excellent piece of Carling captaincy; he knew we had it covered.

It was the first sending-off at Test level on the advice of an assistant referee; it was also an easy call. It was gratuitous and avoidable serious foul play; France were driving over and past the prone Bayfield when the downward stamp was delivered. For good measure, another blow was delivered with a backwards-heel motion.

There was huge trust between match officials in those pre-TMO days (not that there isn't today, it's just that then we didn't have an opportunity to have a second look on the big screen). So when I told Hilditch what had happened and that it was a clear sending-off offence, he simply said, 'Right, I'll go and get him.' That conversation took less than a minute and compared very favourably, I'd suggest, to the long-drawn-out processes we often see today.

This meant that France had to re-jig their front row, with back-row Jean-François Tordo moving up. Up against that mighty English front row of Jason Leonard, Brian Moore and Jeff Probyn, this makeshift arrangement was always going to be in trouble.

Next, a scrum broke up in complete disarray with punches thrown by both front rows, after it appeared that Moscato had led with his head. Hilditch read the riot act, and was very clear in his instructions. There could be no more of it. But as the scrum engaged for the second time, Moscato clearly head-butted Probyn. Again, the ref was left with absolutely no choice; Moscato was sent off. Determined not to leave the field of play, Philippe Saint-André had to escort him off the pitch.

For the record, England left the field as winners by the perfectly palindromic scoreline of 31–13.

The disciplinary panel met immediately after the match and both French players were suspended for six months; neither would be selected to play for their country again. Moscato had 'previous', as they say, and when asked to explain his record he said that he'd been sent off for 'nervousness'. On further questioning, we weren't surprised to learn that it was not Moscato who was nervous. No, he said, it was the referee who got nervous and sent him off.

When news of the length of the suspensions filtered back to the hotel, some members of the French Federation were incensed and the normally enjoyable evening was not particularly pleasant. The security escort off the pitch was a good idea, but we didn't expect to need one at the dinner too.

On our arrival back in Dublin we learned that the French Federation had reviewed events, and actually extended the length of suspensions, on a *sine die* basis.

When we returned the following year for France v Wales, the last match I reffed in Paris, sincere apologies were forthcoming and we were treated royally throughout the weekend, particularly at the post-match dinner after a 26–10 French victory.

In an interesting postscript to the 1992 match, Vincent Moscato went on to have a very successful career as a sports media personality, hosting his own show. He has also had a lot of acting success, including in the stunning *36 Quai des Orfèvres* with Gérard Depardieu and Daniel Auteuil in the leading roles.

It must have been all of 15 years later that I bumped into him on Boulevard Raspail, near Montparnasse. We had walked past each other, and both had stopped, unsure, and looked back – 'Yes, it's you.' We both grinned. We had an enjoyable chat and, as we said our goodbyes, he good-humouredly told me to tell 'Heeldeetch' that he was thinking of forgiving him. Parole for the referee, after only 15 years, seems fair enough to me.

The family in Dartry, circa 1956.
Top (left to right): Owen and Adrienne.
Bottom (left to right): Betty, Ross, Linda and Eddie

Jean Lawton and Eddie Doyle in Bordeaux, circa 1960

Holiday home in Ardamine, circa 1965

Left: Working at Château Cantenac Brown, 1967

Right: The future referee breaks out of defence, 1967

Above: UCD Freshman XV, a motley crew perhaps, but winners of the league. The whistler-to-be is bottom left, 1967–68

Right: 'The dirtiest match I ever reffed'; Dave Burnett dispatches Wales' Paul Ringer, February 1980

IRFU interprovincial championship, Ravenhill, Belfast, October 1982

SECRETARY & TREASURER
R. FITZGERALD.
TELEPHONE DUBLIN 684601
TELEGRAPHIC ADDRESS,
"FOOTBALL. DUBLIN"
TELEX 90526

IRISH RUGBY FOOTBALL UNION.
62, LANSDOWNE ROAD.
DUBLIN. 4

ref RF/SMacS

28th Nov. 1983

Wales v. Scotland 21st Jan. 1984
Cardiff

Dear Owen,

Please note that the WRU is being advised of appointments, including you, as follows in respect of the above match:

Referee: Mr. O.E.Doyle
Sub-Referee & Touch Judge: Mr. D.I.H.Burnett
Touch Judge: Mr. J.R. West

The WRU will communicate with you.

Please make your own travel arrangements and claim cost from this office.

Yours sincerely,

R.FITZGERALD
Secretary

O.E. Doyle Esq
D.I.H.Burnett Esq
J.R. West Esq

Wales v Scotland, Cardiff.
The long-awaited formal
letter – my first cap,
January 1984

Wales v Australia, Cardiff Arms Park, November 1984.
There's no place on Earth quite like it

Newport v New Zealand, October 1989. One of ten
All-Black tries that day, not an enjoyable match to referee

Oxford v Cambridge, Twickenham, December 1990.
Plenty of drama before, during and after the 'Varsity match

France v England, Parc des Princes, February 1992.
Now a pundit, Martin Bayfield lies prone in Paris; a French boot was involved

France v England, Parc des Princes, February 1992

Left: Grégoire Lascube is sent off by Stephen Hilditch
as a result of the Bayfield incident

Right: Vincent Moscato follows Lascube shortly afterwards,
dismissed following a head-butt at a scrum

Dave McHugh making things clear to
Paddy Johns and Trevor Brennan, August 1999

South Africa v New Zealand, August 2002,
Dave McHugh, after he was attacked by a spectator

Chapter Eight

13 October 1991

Fiji v Romania in Brive
(Would Cup pool stages)

It was a howitzer.

Fijian full-back Opeti Turuva had fielded a long Romanian clearance kick just inside the opposition half. Taking a few steps forward, he unleashed an enormous drop kick – it was from just short of the 10-metre line, and five metres in from touch.

The ball went high over the bar, just inside the top of the post. The referee was perfectly positioned, if I say so myself – I had realised what was about to come my way, and hadn't budged from the point of the clearing kick.

Owen Doyle

It was an easy task to run in from where I was standing, and to be certain the kick was good, even though it was tight as could be. What a pleasure it was to witness.

● ● ●

From time to time, as far back as the 1950s, the idea of a rugby World Cup had surfaced. But it did not get sufficient support until 1985, when a majority of the then eight member unions who constituted the International Rugby Board (IRB) voted it in by a margin of six to two. It was a very well-researched joint proposal from New Zealand and Australia, and the timing for the first RWC in 1987 was to avoid any clash with the Olympic Games, and soccer's own World Cup. Only Scotland and Ireland did not support the idea, and while that might seem to have been lacking in vision, it was consistent with their views on keeping the sport amateur. This was seen as a first step towards professionalism, and so it proved to be.

The RWC has turned out to be not only a wonderful rugby tournament, but a truly great sporting event. It has also been a financial success of staggering proportions.

Having become established on the international scene a number of years before the first World Cup was due to be held, I had hopes of making the panel for that inaugural tournament, but alas it was not to be. Instead, Ireland's representatives would be my Leinster colleague Dave Burnett and Ulster's Stephen Hilditch.

Burnett was an absolute shoo-in, and probably the best referee in the world at that time. He was the go-to man for many big matches, including the previous year's Five Nations XV v Overseas Unions XV at Twickenham, which was the showpiece fixture of the IRB's centenary celebrations. Those teams were an extraordinary array of the very best talent around, with Ireland's Donal Lenihan captaining the Five Nations in a 13–32 defeat.

The second place was pretty much a toss-up between Stephen Hilditch and myself, and he got the call. My aversion to long-haul flying quickly dampened any feelings of disappointment, and the balance of one referee from each side of the border had a very appropriate feel to it. The three of us had a really enjoyable evening together before they went on their way. And with Burnett due to retire at the tournament's end, I already had my eye on the next tournament, four years hence.

The Irish players, led by team manager Syd Millar, departed, their main purpose being to see how far they could go, but really intent on enjoying the experience. Millar was a legend of the game, having coached Ireland (1974–75) and the Lions on their 1974 tour of South Africa. It'd be easier to list the things he did not do in rugby than to actually write down what he achieved; it's not just Ireland who owe the Ballymena man a huge debt, it's each and every union. His later years as chairman of the International Rugby Board, from 2003 to 2007, were progressive and set out a very clear strategic plan for the future of the game. He, along with his predecessor, Welshman Vernon Pugh, were the first true visionaries. We could do with both of them now.

In his playing career, he was an impossibly strong first-choice loose-head for Ireland from 1958 to 1970, and toured with the Lions in 1959, 1962 and 1968, playing in a total of nine Tests. It's worth bearing in mind that these were the 'old-fashioned' long tours of over three months, encompassing 25 or 30 matches. In addition to receiving a British knighthood, France awarded Sir Sydney Millar their most prestigious decoration, *la Légion d'honneur*.

The now top-rated rugby pundit, Donal Lenihan was captain of a terrific team, which included such household names as McNeill, Rainey, Ringland, Bradley, Glennon, Anderson, Dean, Ward, Mullin, Orr, Mathews and Derek McGrath, who would later become the first, and first-class, CEO of European Rugby Cup Ltd.

Sadly missing from the squad was Nigel Carr, whose career had been ended en route to a pre-tournament training session in that horrific IRA bomb blast that took the lives of Lord Justice Maurice and Lady Cecily Gibson.

Having had a wonderful playing career with Ireland and also the Lions, Mick Doyle had taken over as coach from Willie John McBride, leading Ireland to a rare Triple Crown and Five Nations championship in 1985. His famous 'give it a lash' style was the forerunner of the recently much-feted 'keep the ball alive'.

Mick was no stranger to fun and enjoyment, and no one in that squad was looking forward more than him to experiencing the first World Cup, and experiencing it to the fullest, as he did with everything in life. But the gods were conspiring against him and, on the flight, he began to feel unwell. On arrival, he tried to ignore the symptoms, before being hospitalised, where a heart attack was diagnosed.

Syd Millar and George Spotswood took over the coaching for a week while Doyle received treatment at an Auckland hospital, but he was back at the coalface before Ireland had started their pool games. A quip in a long-distance phone call from then-Taoiseach Charlie Haughey, that the coach was 'only suffering Guinness withdrawal pangs', suggested that Doyle's reputation as the life and soul of the party went before him.

In the pool stages, Ireland lost narrowly to Wales, but beat Tonga and Canada. These results meant a quarter-final against Australia, who duly won 33–15. Ireland's annoying habit of getting no further than the quarters had begun.

On a much more enjoyable and amusing note, this World Cup was famous for the dilemma Ireland faced in choosing what national anthem to play. No one had thought this through, and it was long before Phil Coulter was commissioned to come up with 'Ireland's Call'. While everyone takes great pride that rugby in Ireland is a 32-county game, it does mean there are citizens from two jurisdictions on the team.

Those from north of the border are happy enough for 'Amhrán na bhFiann' to be played at Lansdowne Road and to stand correctly to attention, if not necessarily going as far as singing it with any great enthusiasm. But the union considered it inappropriate that this should be the anthem of the Ireland team for the World Cup and that, therefore, we would not have one. But the team wanted something played, so what would it be?

The best brains in the business were concentrated on this knotty problem, apparently of Gideon proportions. I suppose many tunes were considered – maybe 'There Is An Isle', maybe 'Song for Ireland' or even 'Danny Boy'. But, in the end, there wasn't much consideration at all, as there were few recordings readily available. Someone did have a James Last cassette, however, and one tune on that was deemed acceptable to everyone.

Nevertheless, when the strains of 'The Rose of Tralee' started to echo around Wellington's Athletic Ground ahead of the Wales game, it was to the utter amazement and amusement – and probably a degree of shock and horror as well – of all watching. Many, including myself, presumed it was a mistake by the tournament organisers. You couldn't make it up.

So, love or hate Phil Coulter's opinion-splitting composition, things could be a lot worse.

By mid-June, the tournament had reached the knockout stages and, in Sydney, France and Australia were locked in an epic semi-final.

The score was tied at 24–24 and the lead has already changed hands six times; time was running out. Serge

The Ref's Call

Blanco passed to Patrice Lagisquet, who kicked ahead, France regathered possession and set off on a remarkable inter-passing movement. They got blocked down the right-hand touchline and went left again, fast and hard. The ball went back to Lagisquet, who carried at pace, the move nearly stalled but Laurent Rodriguez picked up and passed to Blanco, who had started the whole thing off. In a trice, he had squeezed over at the left corner, and Australia were out.

That wonderful try was preceded by the ball being won by the forwards and whipped out to the backs. Thirteen French players handled the ball in that magical move, including Blanco and Lagisquet twice each. Both French props, Pascal Ondarts and Jean-Pierre Garuet, also handled in the move, but only to act as important links in keeping the ball in motion.

Today, those players would search for an opponent to charge into, and then the same again, collision after collision.

That result presented an unexpected refereeing dilemma and an unfortunate knock-on effect for Dave Burnett. Australia and New Zealand had staged the tournament, and now the French had ruined the anticipated dream final of the two host nations fighting it out to be the first winner of the coveted Webb Ellis Cup.

The Irishman had looked a lot more than a good bet to referee the final, even before the tournament started. And the semi-final appointments of Australia's Kerry Fitzgerald and Scotland's Brian Anderson only seemed to confirm the thinking that Burnett was heavily pencilled in for it.

But Australia – perhaps not unnaturally – wanted to be represented on the pitch for the decider, and if their team wasn't going to be there, then their referee would. So politics took over and Kerry Fitzgerald was leap-frogged into the match. A very fine referee and a lovely guy, he was embarrassed by this turn of events, but nobody could have expected him to turn it down. Burnett, in true gentlemanly fashion, kept his disappointment to himself.

New Zealand lifted the cup, easily beating France, 29–9. France had, mentally, played their final the previous week. Captained by David Kirk, this All Blacks team also included Sean Fitzpatrick, who would go on to become one of rugby's all-time great captains.

While the international game was clearly the pinnacle of the sport, with the World Cup extending the game's global reach, there were a number of traditional fixtures tied to the amateur ethos that were prized appointments. The annual 'Varsity match between Cambridge and Oxford was one such game, regularly selling out Twickenham. Custom dictated that the two captains would sit down and decide who they would invite to referee, a practice which was sadly discontinued some years ago.

In 1990, Simon Holmes was Cambridge captain, and I had refereed them during their tour of Japan, at the request of Japan RFU Chairman Shiggy Konno. For Oxford, the captain was Irishman Mark Egan of Terenure and Trinity.

I had returned from Tokyo on the same plane as Cambridge,

and, when we disembarked, Holmes shook my hand and said that I would be his pick for the forthcoming 'Varsity encounter. He told me they'd taken bets as to how far into the flight it would be before I would seek out that appointment. We'd all got on well during the tour, but they appreciated that I hadn't even touched on the subject. In fact, it had never crossed my mind; as usual, I was too busy checking out the turbulence on the 13-hour haul from Tokyo to Heathrow.

Back in Dublin, I mentioned it to Egan, and he said that sounded like a good idea, that he'd back it fully. Both Holmes and Egan were true to their word, so I packed my bags again and left for London.

My hotel was in Richmond and Cambridge were billeted nearby. Watching them board their coach as they left, complete with outrider police escort, I was tempted to ask for a lift but, on second thoughts, disembarking at the ground with one of the teams didn't seem a good fit. I ordered a taxi, but still a few kilometres from the ground found myself gridlocked in heavy traffic as the crowd gathered. The London cabbie could offer no indication on an ETA so I paid him off and ran the last stretch. Many referees leave Twickenham in a state of exhaustion, but that's not the recommended state for arrival.

Worse came as I togged out. Inexplicably, I had packed a pair of rugby shorts belonging to my son. I've never had a claim to a 20-inch waist, so these barely came up to my thighs. The solution was to borrow a pair from the Cambridge kitman.

Despite Cambridge being firm favourites, Egan's Oxford ran out winners 21–12, a famous win. There was a hint of offside for one Oxford try, an intercept by USA Eagles winger Gary Hein, which was nearly a major talking point. Cambridge had an overlap, with Tony Underwood free, out to the left on halfway. As the pass went to him, I over-anticipated what would happen next and headed for the corner flag. For a second I was completely unsighted, and when Underwood reappeared, as was expected, there was an immediate problem – he didn't have the ball. And by this time yours truly was heading into the Oxford 22.

Looking back downfield, I could see the back of an Oxford jersey – number 14. It was Hein sprinting into the opposite 22, and over the line to touch down. Clearly, he had intercepted but had he caught it cleanly or had he knocked it on? I didn't have a clue. Well, the faithful old rule is don't give what you haven't seen, and I had not seen a thing, so the try was given. Thankfully, it turned out to be correct, which Hein confirmed to me as he trotted back.

There could be no assistant referee help in this game, the tradition being for the previous year's captains to take on the role, probably for the only time in their lives. I am sure that the Australian international Brian Smith, also capped by Ireland, who did the job that day for Oxford had never done it before. Also, the position of TMO had yet to be created, so a referee in a moment like that was completely alone, for better or for worse, and it might well have been for worse.

Many referees are members of the informal 22-metre

Club, indicating that they have awarded a try from as far away as the 22. In that moment, I became founder, and probably still the only member, of the Halfway Line Club. An overhead picture in *The Times* of London the next day showed Hein crossing for the try, at the same time as my own foot could be seen crossing the halfway line.

The evening was spent at the fabulous Oxford and Cambridge Club in Pall Mall. Trust me, those two great institutions do not know how to do things by half. The next day most of London seemed to have gone back to work as I found myself wandering around Leicester Square, alone and at a loose end. With the December rain fairly tipping down, I noticed a sign pointing to somewhere much more agreeable, and that is how I found the famous Cork & Bottle, probably London's most notable wine bar. As I ordered a glass of wine, several well-suited and very smart-looking businessmen obviously did not have work on their agenda. They turned out to be a group of former Oxford students rolling over from the previous day's match. Knocking back magnums of champagne, they invited me to join them. A rugby equivalent of golf's 19th hole went long into, and past, the afternoon. When, eventually, I emerged back onto the square it was dark and I was trying to remember which city it was.

With Dave Burnett now retired and new kid on the block Brian Stirling with only a few matches under his belt, I was confident of earning a spot at the 1991 World Cup. That said, while it wasn't a surprise to get the call from the IRFU's George Spotswood that summer to confirm my selection, there was certainly a degree of satisfaction that I'd be part of it. Stephen Hilditch was Ireland's other choice, and while the co-hosting by England, France, Ireland, Scotland and Wales meant a lot of travelling, at least the dreaded long-haul flights were avoided. We had an excellent hotel base in Cardiff, and the spirit among the group, managed by the urbane former English international referee (and my one-time assessor) Peter Brook, was excellent.

Brook was a very interesting character, and had just bought himself a spanking new coupé. One day, Welsh referee Derek Bevan needed to pop home for a few hours and cheekily asked for a loan of the car. Brook immediately chucked him the keys, to the general amazement of all, including the new driver. When he returned, Bevan handed back the keys, announcing that 'she pulls a bit at 70 in second gear'. He later confessed to me that he was so terrified of damaging the car that he never got above 20 mph.

One of my best evenings of the tournament was with Bevan. The group were preparing to attend yet another formal reception, but I had excused myself. After they'd departed the hotel, I took the lift to the foyer – armed with a good book, I was planning a quiet meal alone. A Welsh accent surprised me from behind, asking where I thought I was going. It was Bevan; he too had thought of an evening by himself but immediately suggested that we 'go alone together', which of course we did. We talked about everything under the sun, and I don't think I've ever laughed so much; it was a much-needed break from everything rugby. Of course, we are still in touch.

The referees at that tournament included high-powered household names, such as Kerry Fitzgerald, who'd refereed the previous final, Bevan, who would be appointed to this one, and Ed Morrison, who would get the showpiece four years later. And there were others, including David Bishop (NZ), Fred Howard (England) and Jim Fleming (Scotland).

That was a lot of talent. The panel included maybe eight referees who could easily have done a quarter-final match at least. Despite knowing all of that, there was still a touch of disappointment when the match allocation was announced and my pool games consisted of Italy v USA and Romania v Fiji.

Nevertheless, I was, after all, at the tournament and determined to enjoy my two games, and the whole experience of a World Cup.

The tournament was scheduled to start at Twickenham on 3 October, but for the officials it kicked off a week before in a match watched by very few spectators. Kenny Rowlands was Welsh referee manager at the time, and he had organised a challenge between two youth teams, so that the referees could see how best to get consistency of interpretation across all the games. New Zealander Keith Lawrence volunteered to ref it, the rest of the group sitting in the stands to observe proceedings.

Things had barely started when the most extraordinary

brawl broke out; every player joined the fracas, wild punches were thrown at will, it was awful. Lawrence did very well to bring things under control, telling the players that he hadn't travelled all the way from New Zealand for that sort of nonsense.

We were all pretty shocked, except Rowlands, who was grinning broadly from ear to ear; it turned out he had spent several days choreographing the mayhem. We had all been duped, no one had cottoned on, so well had he organised the punch-up. When he explained things, the match continued peacefully for its originally intended purpose.

Strict instructions had been issued not to let players go off their feet at the breakdown, and the opening match, England v New Zealand, saw Scottish referee Jim Fleming put down a marker for the rest of the tournament. Bevan and Fleming eventually finished their careers with a truly remarkable four World Cups under their respective belts.

Another quirk of rugby law was that the practice of lifting players in the lineout was at that time illegal, and we were told to be extremely hard and to penalise it immediately. It's difficult to believe that that was the case then, given what has become the norm since the law change in 1995.

The biggest shock in 1991 was Western Samoa's win over Wales (16–13), which dumped the co-hosts out of the tournament. That match was laced with controversy when Samoa were awarded a very dubious try by French referee Patrick Robin, where it appeared that the defending Robert Jones had beaten To'o Vaega to the touchdown.

The Ref's Call

It was well before anyone had even thought about a TMO, and the decision had a high degree of difficulty; Robin could only give it as he saw it.

The score was 3–3 at the time and Wales still had plenty of time to win the match, but the physicality, strength and hard, chest-high tackling of the Samoans was overwhelming, causing three Welsh players – Phil May, Tony Clement and Richie Collins – to be forced off with injury.

My tournament began on 5 October in Otley, West Yorkshire, where Italy overcame USA by a somewhat flattering 30–9 scoreline in a really enjoyable contest. Peculiarly, given what was to come in Brive, it was also another day of the drop kick. The wonderful Argentinian-born Italian out-half Diego Domínguez seemed very determined to land one. He had a go at three but, surprisingly, for a man of his great kicking ability, none of them hit the target. On the other hand, he had a 100 per cent record off the tee, six from six – two conversions and four penalties.

Peter Brook had turned up to watch, no doubt running his eye over who might be in line for greater things if some of his designated top men were injured or had a poor performance.

It's a tribute to them that they did not, so my spell in the middle aptly finished in France with an enjoyable clash between Romania and Fiji, which included that famous drop goal by the latter's full-back Opeti Turuva.

One of the longest in World Cup history, it was also the third successful Fijian drop goal of the afternoon, but their accuracy in kicking from hand was not enough to deny the Romanians, who edged the game 17–15 to finish third in the group. Canada, who had beaten both, were qualifiers behind the French.

France, and myself, now moved on to Paris for a quarter-final with England, a brutal affair in which I was fourth official for New Zealand's Dave Bishop. Before the game, a very high-ranking FFR committee man, Marcel Martin, visited us to wish us well, as was his wont. On this occasion, he left a case of six magnums of champagne in the dressing room in anticipation of victory over the English. It all went wrong for the French and, after the match, the case remained just where he had left it.

We were preparing to leave when our minder suggested that we should take the bubbly, as otherwise it would just be wasted. In a rare moment of total foolishness, we stuffed the bottles into our kitbags; we had barely completed the task, just about managing to close the zips, when Martin returned. He stared at the empty, ripped-open case, and his gaze then fell onto our bags, with the outline of the bottles sending out the clearest of messages as to their new location. He smiled, and said that if anyone knew where his champagne had disappeared to, perhaps we could find it, and return it to him later.

I am sure there is a word out there for more than total mortification, and that's precisely the state we were in when we knocked on his hotel-room door. Beaming, he thanked us for our endeavours, opened a bottle which he had prepared earlier, and we had a very pleasant pre-dinner drink. Talk about *savoir-faire*.

The following day, Hilditch and I were due in Lille to assist English referee Fred Howard for New Zealand's quarter-final match against Canada. Howard had justifiably earned the sobriquet of 'Fearless Fred' for his involvement in several high-profile sendings-off – particularly his correct dismissal for a stamp in Murrayfield by Frenchman Alain Carminati in 1990, the year the Scots won their third Grand Slam.

As we headed by car, northeast from Paris, the rain descended in bucket-loads. We were being driven by our usual 'minder', the ever-affable Frenchman Michel Alguacil; he had the windscreen wipers going full blast, but the lack of visibility was truly scary, and we were very happy to arrive in one piece.

The match itself was one I'll remember for blood, sweat and tears, and that all happened before the kick-off. Howard had checked the boots of both teams and, perhaps because of the conditions, New Zealand had opted for 18-millimetre-length studs. Problem was, they weren't legal, 15mm being the maximum allowed at that stage. Having pleaded hard for leniency, the All Blacks, mainly through the good offices of their legendary manager John Sturgeon, finally agreed to change them to the appropriate length. There was just about enough time to do so.

So their baggage master, the ever-affable Englishman Graham Short, stepped forward, armed with the correct studs, plus a pliers and a wrench. Don't forget that each boot had a minimum of six studs, and with 15 players plus replacements, there was a hell of a lot of work ahead of him. When Hilditch and I did the final check shortly before kick-off, New Zealand, all rebooted, were ready to take the field. Short sat in the middle of the dressing-room floor, surrounded by the abandoned hardware, fingers bleeding, sweating profusely, tears of relief in his eyes. It was undoubtedly one of the greatest, although unheralded, feats of that World Cup.

For the record, New Zealand weren't overly affected by the shorter studs, winning 29–13, scoring five tries. And, thankfully, 'Fearless Fred' wasn't called upon to be, well, fearless.

The match of this tournament took place in Lansdowne Road, Ireland v Australia – and another, particularly heartbreaking, quarter-final exit for the men in green. Who will ever forget Irish flanker Gordon Hamilton outpacing David Campese over 40 metres to score what we all thought would prove to be the winning try, and put Ireland 18–15 ahead with just five minutes left. It was a truly wonderful try, greeted by one of the loudest roars ever heard at Lansdowne Road; surely we would win now. But, no. As the match was just about over, Ireland failed to find touch, the otherwise excellent Rob Saunders being the villain of the piece.

Moments later, Australia broke up the right-hand side, Michael Lynagh brilliantly collected a Campese inside pass, and touched down just outside the old Wanderers pavilion,

18–19. It was cruel, and this time only the sound of silence was left to echo around the ground.

The team were coached by former Irish and Lions captain Ciaran Fitzgerald. He is perhaps best remembered for his rousing and challenging cry of 'Where's your f***ing pride?' when Ireland were wilting in their 1985 Triple Crown bid at Lansdowne Road. That team found that pride and drove deep into the English 22, giving Michael Kiernan the opportunity to drop kick his famous goal that clinched the crown.

Australia beat their old enemy New Zealand in the semi-final, and did enough to win the trophy in the final against England, which was refereed by the splendid Derek Bevan. It was Bevan, a master of the one-liner, who remarked after the Welsh defeat to Western Samoa that it was just as well Wales weren't playing the whole of Samoa – which, of course, they were.

During the tournament, I heard a whisper that both myself and Hilditch had been the subject of pretty negative performance reviewing from a certain assessor. These guys held a lot of sway and could directly influence appointments. I told Stephen what I'd heard, which he found hard to believe. In order to be sure, I borrowed the driver's keys to our team coach where the assessor had left his briefcase, and removed a few sheets of his notes, which I carefully replaced later.

The proof of the pudding is in the eating, as they say. The assessor's description of Fiji v Romania bore little rela-tion to what I remembered; it seemed like we'd been at a different match in terms of how he viewed some of my calls.

The books were somewhat balanced by another assessor, Australian John Miner, who was much more supportive in his views of us, and his opinion at selection meetings would have been held in high regard. Things did, then, take a turn for the better as Hilditch was deservedly rewarded with the third-place play-off, now known as the bronze final. You could say it was a different type of whistleblowing to the normal, everyday stuff. A year or so later, the assessor did have the guts to offer a sincerely meant apology, which was accepted with no reservations whatsoever, and we shook hands over a pleasant drink with no lasting hard feelings.

Shortly after the tournament was over and we'd all returned home, I got a very-early-morning phone call from David Burnett – our Australian colleague Kerry Fitzgerald had collapsed and died at the very young age of 43. One of the fittest and trimmest of referees, he had, of course, handled the 1987 final, and this time around the England v Scotland semi-final. As the rain appropriately beat down in Dublin, we could barely speak at this terrible news, which deeply shocked and saddened the whole rugby world.

Dubray Books
Unit 12
Swan Shopping Centre
Rathmines, Co Dublin
Tel: (01) 497 9722
rathmines@dubraybooks.ie

21-12-22 11:21   SALE 1 418461   0309
You were served by: Fionn

PRODUCT   QTY   VAT

REFS CALL: MEMOIR OF A   1   Z

Chapter Nine

19 November 1994

*Scotland v South Africa in Murrayfield
(First Test of the Springboks' tour
of Britain and Ireland)*

As we prepared to tog out and do all the pre-match bits and pieces, which by now had become second nature, we were absolutely staggered at the sheer physical size of the South African team; they were huge.

Thankfully, apart from sorting out one mini dust-up, there wasn't too much for me to do during the match except keep quiet and stay out of the way. The second requirement was harder than the first, but I just about managed it.

At the start of the second half, I realised that my refereeing innings was coming to the end. The players appeared to have *suddenly got much faster, and it seemed like the pitch had somehow become much, much bigger.*

It felt like one era was ending and another beginning, both for the sport and for myself.

• • •

Having been excluded from the first two World Cups, the end of the apartheid regime in South Africa saw them readmitted to the international rugby fold in 1992 and, as part of their sporting rehabilitation, the country was awarded the hosting of the 1995 tournament. In preparation, they had travelled for a tour of Britain and Ireland in the autumn of 1994 and I had been selected to referee their opening Test against Scotland in Murrayfield.

During the week, I had felt oddly flat about the match, instead of having that wonderful feeling of anticipation that had always been the forerunner of these big games. To be honest, the lack of motivation had begun to creep in earlier in the club season but I'd assumed that this would sort itself out when we all arrived in Edinburgh, given the profile of this fixture. However, the flat feeling persisted and was impossible to shake off.

The morning of the match couldn't have been more different from my first international experience in Wales a decade earlier. Very strangely, I could not get it into my head that there was a Test match coming up in a few hours, with what seemed like zero adrenaline running through my veins.

Their absence from the international stage meant that I had never refereed South Africa before, so they were the only team of the traditional eight rugby powers I had yet to officiate. This was akin to completing the set, so to speak, but I found myself distracted by the size and shape of the players, which was of a different magnitude to what I'd seen before and, in hindsight, an indicator of where the sport was headed.

The bulk of that Springbok squad would go on to lift the World Cup the following year. Very sadly, illness and untimely deaths have since visited far too many of the team, including the fabulous scrum-half Joost van der Westhuizen who passed away in 2017, aged 45, suffering from motor neurone disease; also, flanker Ruben Kruger died aged 39, after a previously diagnosed brain tumour returned. The two iconic wings Chester Williams (then, their only non-white player) and James Small both passed away from heart failure in 2019, at the terribly young ages of 49 and 50 respectively.

The match would also see the opening of the new Murrayfield stadium with the rebuilt west stand it included a 100-metre running track down the side of the pitch which put the spectators sitting there at quite some distance from the action. I am sure there's a reason for that track, but there's no doubt that this very fine stadium would have been better without it.

Scotland had not played well in the preceding Five Nations, a 6–6 draw with Ireland being their best result, and they came in bottom of the table and picked up the wooden spoon in the process.

But, on paper, the team looked somewhat better than those results, particularly in the backs, which included the Hastings brothers Gavin and Scott, and a strong half-back pairing of Derrick Patterson and Craig Chalmers.

Nonetheless, the opposition looked stronger in nearly every position and, led by François Pienaar, they outplayed Scotland completely. The immense forwards, including Os du Randt, Rudolf Straeuli and Mark Andrews, laid the foundations for a very convincing, and never-in-doubt, victory. Tries came regularly, two from van der Westhuizen, and one each for Chester Williams, Pieter Muller and Rudolf Straeuli. Scotland replied to those five with just one of their own from Tony Stanger in a final scoreline of 34–10 to the Boks.

It had been a strange struggle for me to get 'into' the match. I had a sort of detached feeling, caused undoubtedly by the zero-adrenaline factor, which essentially made my decision to finish at the end of the season quite an easy one. Better not to wait for the axe to fall; getting out before it does can be tricky but is unquestionably the best way to go.

The Springboks remained undefeated on that tour, until the Barbarians beat them 34–10 at Lansdowne Road in their final match. Refereed by Derek Bevan, ably assisted by Dave McHugh, it was a very physical encounter, with Ireland's Simon Geoghegan scoring a vital try in the Baa-Baas' win.

Less than a year later, that Springbok team would provide a seminal moment for rugby and for all of sport. The 1995 Rugby World Cup was the first major event in South Africa after apartheid had ended, and it was also the first time that the competition was played in a single nation.

By then, I was no longer a contender and Stephen Hilditch, once again, and Dave McHugh from Cork, were Ireland's referee representatives. It was Stephen's third World Cup and Dave was to go on to have a stellar career, but was perhaps a tad fortunate to travel ahead of Ulster's Brian Stirling.

It's impossible to forget the joyous scenes after the final when President Nelson Mandela, bedecked in a Springbok jersey, handed over the Webb Ellis Cup to François Pienaar. They had beaten New Zealand – with an extra-time drop goal by Joel Stransky – by just 16–13, in a try-less match.

Actually, there probably had been a South African try, but referee Ed Morrison had been unsighted when Ruben Kruger appeared to have touched down. Ed was a terrific referee but he very candidly admitted as much later.

There was huge controversy afterwards when it was revealed that many New Zealand players had gone down with food poisoning some 48 hours before the match, and they might not have been able to field a team if the match had been scheduled for the day before. All sorts of conspiracy theories emerged, including blaming it all on poisoned water served up by a waitress known as 'Suzie'.

Nobody ever managed to solve the mystery, or prove that it was a deliberate act, but the suspicions will linger for ever.

Ireland, under coach Gerry Murphy and captain Terry Kingston, snuck out of the pool stage with a one-point win over Wales, 24–23. We had beaten Japan but lost to New Zealand in the other matches, so that single point got us to the quarter-finals, where France had an emphatic, 36–12 victory. It was a disappointing performance and no excuses were made. It was the last Irish team to take to the field as amateurs in a World Cup, and that was as notable as it got.

New Zealand had beaten England in the first semi-final, 45–29; an excellent match, with 10 tries in total. What a great honour for Ireland's Stephen Hilditch, and he refereed it very well, with a light and sensible touch. It will be remembered, more than anything, for the performance of a 20-year-old New Zealander, Jonah Lomu, who was an absolute sensation, running in four of the All Blacks' six tries. The standout moment came when he went over, and through, England's Mike Catt before touching down. It was a very brave attempt to stop what resembled a runaway train by full-back Catt, who was appointed Ireland attack coach after RWC 2019.

In the second semi-final, South Africa got the better of France, very marginally, 19–15. The match was played in the worst possible conditions, with large pools of water lying on the surface. The attempts to remove the surface water – a group of local women sweeping the pitch with brooms – were both hilarious and farcical. The game just about went ahead but probably shouldn't have, and the result was in doubt until the final moments.

With two minutes left on the clock, Abdel Benazzi ploughed towards the South African line for what all of France thought was the winning try. But was the ball held up? Was it short of the line? Was it a try? Again, no TMO, and while the well-positioned referee, Derek Bevan, ruled it out, many thought Benazzi had scored. Another moment of high drama.

If Stransky hadn't kicked the winning points in extra-time, the match, which had no tries, would have been decided by awarding victory to the team with the least number of red cards over the course of the tournament; that would have been New Zealand. Dave McHugh's red card to the Boks' James Dalton in the match against Canada would have effectively decided who took home the cup. Mercifully, that did not come to pass.

At the post-final banquet, the South African Rugby Union President Louis Luyt, presented Bevan with a gold watch for his semi-final performance. Bevan was suitably embarrassed and promised that it would be auctioned for charity.

A presumably 'tired and emotional' Luyt then claimed that, now that South Africa had won the World Cup, the rugby world at last had its true champions, emphasising that had they been allowed to play in the two first editions, they would have won them too. Such was the tenor and content of Luyt's speech, defeated New Zealand captain Sean Fitzpatrick led his side out of the room, followed by both England and France, who were in turn accompanied by the referees and their selectors. The 'World in Union' it was not.

But as my career wound down to its natural ending, I could look back without an ounce of regret. Not quite how the 10-year-old boy had imagined things when mesmerised by those black-and-white images on the family TV, but he had, after all, reached the international rugby stage.

A stage that was now preparing for the biggest change since the founding of the original Rugby Football Union in 1871.

Chapter Ten

27 August 1995

Merrion, Dublin 4
(The day rugby union went professional)

I was thinking of an early night, when the phone rang.

'I told you so,' said a Cork accent: Dave McHugh, aka 'Macker' to his friends.

What was it this time, I wondered. 'Told me what?'

'They've only gone and done it,' he said. 'The game's going professional.'

When I realised that he wasn't pulling my leg, a favoured pastime of his, the rest of the evening was taken up with calls zipping backwards and forwards. The Irish position had always been that it should remain amateur, and any conversations I had with Syd Millar and others confirmed that this was a strongly held position.

Everybody was trying to get a handle on what changes would come about, what sort of money would need to be spent to pay players. That, I knew, would come first, and then the Union would have to be prepared to fork out for referees. But how, when or how much – I had no idea. But I knew things would never be the same again.

• • •

In August 1995, the International Rugby Board held a critical three-day meeting in the elegance of the Ambassador Hotel in Paris. There was a controversial, but vitally important, motion on the agenda – 'pay for play', the move to professional status for the sport of rugby union.

The IRFU were represented by Syd Millar and Tom Kieran. They did not like the look of what they saw when they gazed into their crystal ball so the Irish position was to vote 'against', meaning the game should continue in its purely amateur form. However, they had misread the tea leaves. There had been a growing swell of opinion coming from the southern hemisphere that the change had to be made, and this had started to gain very serious traction in the north.

All involved were becoming increasingly fearful of the

The Ref's Call

Australian multimillionaire Kerry Packer, who had previously transformed cricket by establishing his own World Series. And now he was turning his attention to rugby union, and was supportive of a plan by the newly founded World Rugby Corporation (not to be confused with World Rugby, the name adopted by the IRB nine years later) to establish a breakaway global championship. This was led by former Wallaby Ross Turnbull, who piqued the interest of many of the game's top players. In fact, many had indicated that they now believed there was so much money being generated, that the players deserved to share in the spoils, which included growing sponsorship and television-rights payments. The threat to the unions was palpable. Packer would need about 900 players to build his franchises, and the strong word on the street was that there were about half that number ready to sign, if not already signed up.

While Packer's plan eventually came to nought, it was clear that the writing was on the wall for the amateur era. The players were the ones creating the wealth, and doing nothing would only aid the very real and existing threat of the Packer roadshow. South African Rugby Union President Louis Luyt may not have been everybody's cup of tea, but he was strong in his opposition to Packer, warning players that transferring out would result in them never again pulling on the Springbok jersey. Luyt was key in persuading SA players to support, and stick with, the union. And this despite the fact that SA captain François Pienaar, who had lifted the World Cup that June, had been firmly aligned to the Australian media mogul.

All other issues apart, it was pretty clear that some form of payments were already being made to players in several unions, and had been for some time. There were various types of 'boot money' payments in Wales, and probably elsewhere as well, where international players were paid for wearing the boots of various manufacturers. Other players had envelopes left in their kitbags or boots while they showered. Everybody turned a Nelsonian blind eye. At the same time, many top French players listed their occupation as 'PR consultant'.

There is no doubt that the breakaway threat really got the unions moving, as the realisation grew that there was no way back from professionalism. A game-changer in all of this was the mega-deal, announced by Luyt, that Rupert Murdoch's News Corporation was willing to put up $550 million in a new arrangement with SANZAR, the partnership of the South Africa, New Zealand and Australia unions which came into being around the same time.

And there was also another threat on the horizon that couldn't be ignored. The already professional code, rugby league, had broken away in a similar row over paying players exactly 100 years before and was now offering big salaries, particularly in Australia. This Murdoch deal was the killer blow to Packer, and it would mean that SANZAR would continue to control the game in the southern hemisphere. Very importantly, some key players, such as Sean

Fitzpatrick and Jonah Lomu, also signed up with their own union.

One of the most influential voices in Welsh and global rugby, barrister Vernon Pugh, also saw that the amateur system, perhaps more 'shamateur' by now, was no longer fit for purpose, and he tellingly described it as 'a dam that can no longer hold water'. Pugh would steer professionalism through its very early days, and he was also fully involved in the setting up of the Heineken Cup. His sad and early death from cancer, aged only 57, robbed rugby of one its most astute brains.

However, Pugh's belief that the professional game would continue the amateur ethos of the sport has not stood the test of time. Syd Millar's oft quoted 'It's gone' when the deal went through has proved, for many, to be a lot closer to the mark.

Not everybody was prepared, though, for the dawning of this new age of professionalism. Tom Kiernan and Vernon Pugh had been eyeing up the idea of a European Cup for some time, and very astutely knew that it was in the best interests of the game and the unions, that the latter should own such a tournament rather than the clubs.

So an emergency call went out to Dublin for IRFU rugby administrator George Spotswood to travel to Paris. There he, Kiernan and Frenchman Marcel Martin started working on the nuts and bolts of how the new tournament would work. Incredibly, they had it up and running in no time under the auspices of European Rugby Cup (ERC), and Heineken came on board as sponsors.

Dublin solicitor Peter Boyle was also brought in as a director of the new ERC body. The Trinity club stalwart brought a wealth of experience, having been elected the youngest president of the Leinster branch of the IRFU in 1983–84, with the presidency of the union coming his way in the 2006–07 season, along with a very successful stint on the International Rugby Board.

The possibility of the clubs doing something off their own bat had been real, and that might have eventually led to a divisive power struggle. The foresight of the likes of Kiernan and Pugh avoided any such scenario, and although no English or Scottish teams played in the inaugural Heineken Cup tournament, they were on board for the second edition in 1996–97.

Nobody can imagine what rugby union would look like today if the Murdoch deal had not come along and Packer had been able to deliver on his non-union championship. But we can clearly see that money has made a colossal difference to how the game is played. The first thing to disappear was the 'Corinthian' spirit which always imbued the sport – that the taking part was as important as the result. This ran through the game from the lowest level right up to international level. Rugby is complicated in its playing structure and laws – and now it would be played for money. It was a change that proved to be a huge financial burden for unions, and a huge cost to the way the game was to be played and refereed.

It was now pretty obvious that if winning was the only

thing that mattered, then attitudes would change. And change they have, hardened to a point where referee error is simply not tolerated. Jobs are on the line; winning tournaments, or at least finishing high up the table, is all it's about now, and that brings inevitable pressure on all participants: players, coaches and referees. It's not perhaps quite as cut-throat yet as soccer, but coaches know that failure to deliver good performances and results will lead to them being shown the door.

In France, the movement of coaches is perhaps greater than anywhere else. Several top coaches have been around quite a few clubs in a relatively short space of time. One of the best, Christophe Urios, has been to five teams since 2005, albeit including two stints with Castres. Jono Gibbes, five clubs since 2008, which included stints at both Leinster and Ulster, although the latter turned out to be a short stay.

It was all a very far cry from that first international of mine, when Scotland narrowly overcame Wales in Cardiff. The then truly exceptional lock forward Bob Norster approached me as we trooped off the pitch.

'Not bad for your first one, thought we might have had a try there at the end, must have been close?'

I assured him it had been close but not close enough.

'Pity, that. See you in the bar.'

I doubt very much if that sort of conversation would take place today. While that's a shame, it was also inevitable.

The problems for referees in the professional era are plentiful, and chief among them is the avoidance of any error. The stakes are so very high, the pressure enormous. The very necessary addition of the TMO has added to the sense that rugby is now refereed with a slide rule.

Quite a few of the sport's greatest moments would have been ruled out by TMO intervention. Yes, there was probably a forward pass in the everlasting wonder try by Gareth Edwards for the Barbarians against New Zealand. While that match goes back to 1973, very few rugby followers of today's, or indeed any, generation have not seen it. Nobody who has will ever forget Cliff Morgan's commentary, still viewable on demand thanks to the wonders of the internet.

Perhaps the greatest Welsh try of all time would similarly have been disallowed – from a kick ahead by Scotland's Andy Irvine, J.P.R. Williams just about got a pass away to Steve Fenwick on the Welsh 22-metre line. Wing Gerald Davies took over in midfield: 'Where did he come from?' wondered commentator Bill McLaren.

Side-stepping fast, Davies sliced through three defenders and offloaded to Phil Bennett. Bennett out to David Burcher on the right-hand touchline; he improvised an overhead one-handed pass inside to Fenwick again who, with a nano-second to play the ball, flicked it further inside, back to Bennett. Acceleration and twinkling feet left the last two defenders sprawling on the ground, grasping at thin air, as he touched down under the posts.

Today, a close TMO examination of those passes might well have deemed one to be forward. Both those matches were refereed by the splendid Frenchman Georges

Domercq, a very happy common denominator. He did not officiate with a slide rule; if he had – and even back then there were some who did – those two magical moments may well have never happened.

Domercq lived in southwest France, in the small commune of Bellocq where he grew vines and was mayor for 43 years. He passed away peacefully in 2021, in his 90th year, having lived those years to their fullest.

Of course we cannot go backwards, as much as some would like to; but those matches emphasise that as the professional game has evolved, much of what made the game so engaging has been lost.

As these seismic developments in the world of rugby were happening, when it came to my 'day job' there were big changes afoot too. By the early 1990s, the wine trade was altering dramatically and the multinationals were buying up many of the proprietary brands, meaning that champagne and cognac houses were being swallowed up at a rate of knots, and the distribution chain of old was breaking down.

Unfortunately, our own business was not immune to these changes sweeping the industry, leaving no option but to wind things down.

To remain in the industry would have meant starting all over again, which did not hold much appeal for me. However, at the same time, rugby's professionalism was creating new opportunities, including in the IRFU, and as one door shut, another was about to open.

It proved to be even more enjoyable than the wine trade.

Chapter Eleven

February 1996

IRFU headquarters,
62 Lansdowne Road, Dublin

Since presenting my proposals I'd heard nothing from them for a long time, but one morning my phone rang. Once again, it was a Cork accent. 'Owen, you've got it.'

The penny didn't drop. 'Got what?' I ventured, wondering if it was Dave McHugh taking the mick as usual.

'Your budget, all of it, now don't screw things up,' said IRFU committee member Tom Kiernan.

I could hear the smile on the other end of the line, which was matched by my own.

• • •

The Ref's Call

When I first walked up the steps of number 62 Lansdowne Road, I really didn't know what lay behind the door. The IRFU must have been receiving some chiding about not having anyone overseeing the referee function.

Other unions were formalising referee structures during the 1980s and early 1990s, and the referee committee would not have wanted to see Ireland left behind, so, eventually, they decided to put a refereeing development position in place, but without any real knowledge of what was involved. They were pretty much the last union to do so.

I'd been sounded out by George Spotswood at a chance meeting during the 1995 Five Nations to see if it was something I might be interested in and, needing a fresh challenge after departing the wine business, the possibility of moving full-time into the game intrigued me. But rather than a coronation, I discovered there was to be an interview process, a daunting prospect given I had spent the previous 20 years as my own boss.

The vote on professionalism was only a matter of weeks away and, despite the IRFU's opposition to the change, I had plenty of thoughts on what might be needed to usher in this new age, should it come to pass. Having prepared assiduously, I came through a completely different kind of selection process than I'd been used to as a referee. Face-to-face interviews were a different beast to the faceless assessor in the stand, but I was given the nod to start as soon as possible. A fortnight after I began, that professionalism bombshell hit, with managing the move away from amateurism now the Union's priority.

As the first into the role, I had a blank canvas, but no paint – in real terms, no budget. Philip Browne, at the time titled IRFU Secretary/Treasurer, was ostensibly in charge of the finance side of things, but the committees still effectively made all the big decisions.

It was not until 1998 that Browne was appointed to the new role of chief executive. He would oversee many changes, including the creation of new departments and a huge increase in staffing levels. The Aviva Stadium project sits proudly as probably his greatest contribution. Browne, like any CEO, may perhaps wish he'd done some things differently, but he left an important and long-lasting legacy on his retirement in 2021.

From my perspective, Browne adopted a policy of non-interference, which was very welcome. On the other hand, his door was always open and his advice when sought – even at short notice or no notice at all – was always given and always useful.

In the engine room of 'number 62' was George Spotswood, the rugby administrator. Extremely affable, patient and helpful, if he didn't know the answer to something, he knew where to find it. It's quite extraordinary to remember that, way back then, the union's employees could be counted on the fingers of one hand, including Anne MacSweeney, his long-time assistant. On several occasions, Spotswood calmed my furrowed and frustrated brow as I tried to extract money from the union, both for development and for paying the referees. Now that the top end of the game was professional, why should unpaid amateurs officiate it? Well, they shouldn't, and most definitely wouldn't, as far as I was concerned.

My first port of call was the UK, to see how they were doing things. The RFU had a long-established referee department run by Steve Griffiths, who would later become the first referee manager with the IRB. Because of the English union's size, and sheer number of referees, it was a different kettle of fish to the Irish scene and, of course, they had a significant budget. But it was a useful visit nonetheless.

The next step was to draw up a business plan, cost it and present it to the two relevant committees, rugby and finance. To me, it was clear that referees being trained formally and compensated would be a worthwhile investment and ultimate benefit of the IRFU.

Under the chairmanship of Connacht's Dr Malcolm Little, the referee committee was totally supportive of the direction I was planning. It was a friendly, businesslike group and there was no interference in the day-to-day running of things; Little's extraordinary memory came in useful too.

The rugby committee, under the leadership of Ken Reid, were also very enthusiastic about my proposals and were astonished that there were so many different sides to officiating. They gave it their full approval, which, I was astonished to learn, was subject to the finance committee agreeing to pay for it. That committee couldn't find time to see me for a couple of months – more frustration.

Eventually, I was summoned. The meeting was held, I think, in the old Jury's Hotel, at about three o'clock in the afternoon. Chaired by Honorary Treasurer Bobby Deacy, who was well known for running a very tight ship, there were upwards of 10 people in the room. I presented the whole thing all over again.

To say that not too many in attendance showed much interest would be overstating matters. A few were reading their newspapers and one or two were trying not to nod off. They obviously knew something I didn't. Deacy turned the proposal down flat – he had bigger player-fish to fry just at that time. Nevertheless, despite my love of animals, if there'd been an available cat, I might well have aimed a kick at it. I was extremely displeased.

Meanwhile, the four provincial referee associations were wondering what I was doing. I'd been in situ for over six months and they'd heard little from me. This refusal of the finance I needed led to several long coffees with George Spotswood and many chats with Malcolm Little. I didn't threaten to leave, although that notion was at the forefront of my mind. Thoughts of that sort have a funny way of delivering themselves – almost self-fulfilling prophecies – but I knew that I had a better chance of getting the cash than anybody else. And, if it wasn't forthcoming, then it

would need a summit meeting to see how a referee department could be developed without any money. One way or
another, there just had to be a solution.

In all organisations, there are movers and shakers, and
Tom Kiernan, Noel Murphy and Syd Millar were the
serious operators in the IRFU at that time. Nobody had
done more for rugby in Ireland. All three had been capped
multiple times for the national team, not to mention the
Lions, for whom Kiernan had been captain.

Whatever pressure they may have applied on the finance
committee, the call from Kiernan finally arrived and, with
funds in place, I could begin in earnest.

So we were up and running, but there were to be two
temporary casualties along the way.

Dave McHugh had just refereed the inaugural Heineken
Cup final, the tournament being contested by teams from
France, Ireland, Italy, Wales and Romania between October
1995 and January 1996. Toulouse had beaten hosts Cardiff
21–18 after extra-time, the first of four Heineken Cups with
coach Guy Novès in charge.

As Ireland's leading referees, he and Alan Lewis, not
unnaturally, wanted 'pay for play', just like the players were
now getting. Having explained that I needed more time to
sort things properly, they continued to push their valid, but
very untimely, claim. The 'bank' could not afford to put
most of its money into just two baskets – even though they
really did have a valid argument. It was more difficult for

McHugh as he had largely wound down his fruit and vege-
table business to concentrate on refereeing, but the bottom
line was that we just couldn't do it at that point, it would
be at least another 12 months before we could put a proper
structure for payment in place.

Malcolm Little and I chatted things over at length and
concluded that we were being pushed too far. The advisory committee, which also then included David Burnett,
Jim Irvine and Michael Reddan, agreed that McHugh
and Lewis would be suspended pro tem from international matches. It was a huge call, but the tail can't wag
the dog.

Little phoned McHugh, and I tried to track down Lewis,
who was on honeymoon in Australia at the time. That took
quite a while, and I just about got him before the jungle
drums started beating, which they did very soon after we
spoke. I knew that not hearing it from the horse's mouth
would have been dreadful. It was clear that he appreciated
the call, even though the news caused a mighty storm in
both Leinster and Munster.

In the latter, there were calls for my head, the immediate
reinstatement of McHugh, and threats of both legal action
and even a referee's strike. The last of these was ominous,
as it would bring all of Munster rugby crashing to a halt.
In situations like this, you have to front up and not hide
behind the castle walls, so off I went. Chatting to McHugh,
I tried to explain that, while it mightn't appear like it, there
was a clear and definite path back, and that I saw this

measure as absolutely temporary. Legal action would put an immovable boulder on the path, as would a strike. Very wisely, he kept his counsel.

Separately, I spoke with the Munster Association of Referees, and they saw the damage a strike would cause – a potential rift with the union which would take years to mend. I also mentioned that if they did go ahead, then the union would implement its plan B, to ensure any strike wouldn't affect rugby in Munster. Naturally, I kept that plan to myself, but said we were confident that it was robust – while, in actuality, it didn't exist.

All in all, the annoyance was very understandable, but everybody saw sense and rugby continued. The enforced gardening leave for McHugh and Lewis did benefit a few others, who had thought that they were not going to make that final step to Test level – Gordon Black (who would go on to eventually succeed George Spotswood), Bertie Smith and Leo Mayne all made it, albeit briefly.

Over the next 12 months, I put together a payment system that was more than acceptable to both McHugh and Lewis; it also included 13 others in tiered contracted panels. This 15-man team really worked, and gave opportunities to potential international referees. They were tiered absolutely on the merits of their own performances, and given every opportunity to move up through the levels. Despite all of the success that would follow, more would not make it than would, but at least everybody got a fair crack of the whip.

All of these were part-time posts, and that went against what was fast becoming the worldwide norm – full-time referees. The tiered system in Ireland still exists, but the top group of three or four have become full-time, an inevitable step given the amount of rugby and the demands on their time. And once McHugh and Lewis were fully back in the fold, they were determined to become among the very best in the game, a status that they would go on to achieve with distinction.

Now that I had secured the funding, my next challenge was the selection of refs. To start, I held my first meeting with the referee committee in Finnstown House in Lucan. It was an eye-opener.

The system till then had been that this committee picked the top eight referees for the All Ireland League, whereas many more were needed. We were joined by a sub-committee of eight, two from each province, all good and honest men. I was astonished to see what happened next. A lot of bartering and horse-trading went on, until a more or less even split emerged from the three main provinces, to reach the required number. Connacht, with far fewer referees, was also included. Of course, merit was part of it, but it needed to be the only part of it.

There were exchange matches between the provinces, where, for example, Leinster referees would go to Ulster and vice-versa, and so forth around the country. But we were never certain that the best guys were getting the trips or if the performance assessments were accurate or, indeed, realistic. The latter were generally overly subjective, and we needed a much more consistent and universal approach. Also included were assessments from a referee's own province, but, of course, we never received a bad one of those. I knew there had to be a better way, and it had to be found.

Many of my good ideas have come to me when I've been shaving and, one sunny morning, the solution appeared out of the bathroom mirror. It was as clear as that morning's sky and, fortunately, it has stood the test of time. It became known as the interprovincial appointment system, IPAS for short.

A referee considered to have All Ireland League potential would never again be judged in his own province; no local assessment would be considered by the IRFU. He or she would do a series of matches around the rest of the country, with a coherent assessment process, inclusive of objective criteria for scoring the referee's performance across the various game areas. It was no longer opinion-based, and the subjectivity of the assessor was pretty much removed and replaced with objective criteria. The long-standing referee sub-committee was disbanded, and while most of its members understood why, one or two tears were shed. Their sole, albeit more important, role now was to be the main drivers behind the new assessment system, and to help train up others into that job.

The individual referees were delighted with a system that

was consistent and transparent; it was also an unexpected motivational tool for them.

For me, the next step was to look at referee development, and performance improvement. The coaching of referees would now become an integral part of the process. Coaching is akin to being the driving instructor; assessing is being the examiner. When they recognise what's going wrong, the coach must have the skillset to know both why it's going wrong and how to fix it. For now, I decided, the referee department would concentrate fully on the coaching end of things.

Gradually, things began to fall into place, and performances across the board really started to improve. A rising tide lifting all boats was never truer and had a very positive effect on referee performances at all levels.

The referee department was growing, and now it even had its own coordinator, Carol Goti. She was the first staff member I recruited, and it was the first in a series of very good choices for that and other roles.

The role of coordinator became too big for one person; the number of matches was growing fast, and there was significant work in liaising with colleagues who were responsible for flights and hotel reservations. The dreaded work, too, of checking expenses had to be done before submitting these to the accounts department. When Carol moved on, Julie Moran and Neysa Herity took over and continued the excellent work. As with Carol, there was never a cross word in either direction; obviously, they all had endless patience. I remember sitting in on Neysa's final interview, and asking the usual, 'Do you have any questions at all which you'd like to put to me?' The unhesitating reply was, 'When can I start?' Much later, she told me that she was certain that her question had blown away any chance of getting the job. But for me, the opposite was true: it had actually sealed the deal for her.

Nobody who is not involved can imagine the immense amount of work that goes on behind the scenes in all departments to ensure that the Ireland team arrive at the right place and time on any given match day. When Ireland run out at, say, Twickenham, their travel and accommodation arrangements will all have had to run like clockwork, as is the case with the match officials. In charge of all of this non-stop logistics were the 'two Janes', Healy and Kilkelly; both of whom had unheard-of levels of patience in dealing with the requirements of a sometimes very needy bunch of referees.

While I was waiting for Deacy to find the key to his money box, I had concentrated on getting the top 50 referees together, which was the first step in our national panel system. And there were all sorts of appointments to be made; for example, we were asked to fill in one of Samoa's matches on their 1996 tour to the UK. One particular match was Samoa v Cambridge, so I called up Graham Crothers, a Belfast surgeon, who had attended Cambridge himself. Needless to say he was thrilled, so off he went. Unfortunately, neither of us thought to 'cry him off' from any other local match which the Ulster branch may have appointed him to referee. It just didn't cross my mind to check things out, but he had been pencilled in to do a Junior Cup final on the same day.

The result of this inept oversight was that as Crothers was getting ready at Cambridge's Grange Road, the Ulster match organisers were getting worried as to his whereabouts. The band was playing, the tents were up, the catering and beer were in place, the teams were togging out. Things went as flat as a pancake when people started to realise there was no referee, and hence no match. The IRFU would later fork out for the whole thing to be rearranged, as George Spotswood poured oil on troubled waters.

The part-time contract system of 15 referees continued to work very well, and while the number of those who reached Test status was 10 men and two women, there were many others who came very close without quite managing the last step. Some of these were more than capable, but the competition was stiff, and Ireland were unlikely to get more than three onto the international stage at any one time, although for several years we did manage to have four. Those were the days.

But I continued to find the committee very useful to run things past, particularly in an informal way over a meal when the official business was out of the way. This committee was the only one which was by invitation and that meant I could, effectively, propose the members, and ensure that only people who would be both positive and challenging at the same time were invited.

Over the years, we had several changes, including the chairman when Malcolm Little, by dint of a surprising vote in the Connacht branch, unfortunately lost his seat at the top table. Many of the subsequent chairmen went on to be president of the IRFU, including Stephen Hilditch. When president-to-be, former international centre Ian McIlrath took on the role, he amusingly wondered aloud how he could do the job when he'd long ago promised himself that he'd never speak to referees. Another, John Callaghan, president in 2009, made a really important, valuable contribution during his time in the chair.

Others on the committee over the years included Tom Aplin, Brian Stirling, Denis Templeton, Bertie Smith and Dave McHugh. The longest-serving then were Irvine and Aplin, who deserve a lot of gratitude for their input. Not so long ago Irvine travelled from Belfast for lunch with Aplin and myself; the wine, banter and the 'insults' flowed.

Overall, I found the small committee to have other benefits too. In an extraordinary incident, a couple of Munster assessors, when excluded from the elite panel, complained in writing to head office about the decision. It had, importantly, been rubber-stamped by the referee committee so was not a maverick, out-of-the-blue call and was actually based on a proposal from the IRB to reduce the overall number of assessors in order to get more consistency. While I certainly did not appreciate their action, I nonetheless headed off to Limerick to meet their own provincial referee committee. Among the complaints levelled were that I had built a golden circle and had surrounded myself with my friends.

Which, of course, I had found to be a much better idea than surrounding myself with enemies. That committee really should have known better.

The outcome of this episode was that the decision stood, despite entreaties that I should change it. The active referees in Munster were upset; they considered that the whole saga would leave them out of consideration for top honours. The opposite happened, and I was true to my word that, wherever the best came from, be it Kerry's Valentia Island or the swankiest house on Dublin's Killiney Hill, it mattered not a jot to me. It was all simply about merit.

About three times a year, it was necessary to report to the full IRFU committee, which was interesting but didn't really achieve very much. I found it better to keep everybody informed by writing and annually updating a set of strategic objectives – in other words, key performance indicators (KPIs) – for the referee department. That also had the benefit of keeping us all firmly focused on where we were going, and challenged us to get there.

The Ref's Call

Every department in any sporting – or business – organisation must surely have such KPIs in place. Without them, there is a clear danger that things become rudderless, the vision lost.

Chapter Twelve

21 September 1997

Brive v Pontypridd in Brive-la-Gaillarde
(Heineken Cup pool stage)

*It began in the Brive in-goal, with what looked like the full
complement of both packs joining in a massive brawl.*

*This sort-of then split up and became four or five different
serious punch-ups going on at the same time.*

*What on earth could a referee do here? The simple answer
is not much at all. He certainly would be a foolish man to
attempt to separate the players, and Eddie Murray was
rightly not going to get closely involved.*

*Instead, he adopted a near-nonchalant approach, and
watched and waited until the fires burned themselves out.*

• • •

The town of Pontypridd was founded on two mining industries, coal and iron. Men who worked and mined these collieries were hewn out of the rocks that came from these deep, deep shafts. Some of them played rugby and, unsurprisingly, none of these men knew what it was like to take a step backwards.

'Ponty' is a proud Welsh club that now plays semi-professional rugby. But before the establishment of the Welsh regional teams who now play in the United Rugby Championship and in Europe, they competed in the Heineken Cup.

Hundreds of kilometres to the south, across the channel, in the heart of France, lies Brive.

During the Second World War, this area was at the centre of France's resistance fighters, including the 'secret army'. So no backward steps here either.

In 1997, Brive were European champions, having beaten Leicester in the final at Cardiff Arms Park, by 28–9. In fact, it was a terrific display by the Frenchmen, who swept their opponents away in a pulsating performance. Welshman Derek Bevan didn't have to travel very far to referee this sparkling encounter.

The following season's competition saw Ponty and Brive drawn in the same pool, and the first match was scheduled for Brive's home ground that September, with Scotsman Eddie Murray the designated referee. Nobody could have forecast what was in the air on what turned out to be one of the most shameful days in the history of not only the Heineken Cup but of the sport of rugby itself.

What is sadly forgotten is that some very good rugby was played. The match went down to the wire and a late push-over try, about which there was some debate, gave victory to Brive by a solitary point, 32–31. Neil Jenkins, the Ponty captain, also let three points go a-begging after missing a kick he would normally get in his sleep.

What the game is remembered for is the brawl to beat all brawls, which came late in the first half. This was as far removed from the quaintly termed 'handbags' as you could wish, or rather not wish, to see.

Not just flailing, meaningless arms, with nothing really connecting, but a 'street' fight which seemed as though it would never stop, and which not one official could put himself in the middle of.

When eventually things quietened down and order was restored, the referee took the only sensible option open to him: a player from each team was dispatched to the sideline for good. In truth, he had a wide choice and could have picked any number of players from either side, but his action did send out a clear message.

So it was that Ponty's New Zealander Dale McIntosh and Lionel Mallier of Brive were the chosen ones; they would later each receive 30 days' suspension.

When the final whistle blew, Ponty were probably the happier of the two teams; they'd lost on the road by a single point and surely they could turn the tables in the return match at their home ground on Sardis Road in just two weeks' time.

But the fighting wasn't over yet, in fact it was only beginning. Le Bar Toulzac is a famous rugby watering hole in Brive, found on Place des Patriotes-Martyrs, which is quite some address for what happened next. There were various reports as to exactly what occurred, depending on whether the information was in French or English, but it's quite enough to say that the bar was absolutely trashed, bottles and chairs flew wild-west style, and much claret was spilled, as both sets of players renewed their violent hostilities.

Having won the match, Brive lost the battle in the bar, both Christophe Lamaison and Philippe Carbonneau suffering broken noses, in a moment which truly shocked the rugby world. The *gendarmes*, of course, intervened and a trio of Welsh players – Dale McIntosh, Phil John and Andre Barnard – were not allowed to return home when their chartered flight left the next morning.

The hierarchy of French rugby demanded that Ponty be thrown out of the tournament and that might have been an option. But one team being dismissed and the other staying would not have been in any way equitable.

And so to the return match in Sardis Road. By accident or design Irishman Gordon Black was the appointed referee, and really it would have been a hard job to pick a better man. During his career, very little fazed Blackie, and he was well prepared and ready for whatever the day might bring. There's no doubt that both teams would have been under strict instruction not to repeat the nonsense in France, but that is never a guarantee of anything.

In the week before the match, Black sat at his office desk as a multitude of journalists tried to make contact with him. 'The *Telegraph* on line one, the *Western Mail* are waiting on line two,' and so on came the messages from reception, so the pressure was undoubtedly mounting.

We met for a beer at the Merrion Inn one evening and our chat revolved around him sticking to his game plan around foul play. He was strong in that area and, at the IRFU, we had full confidence in his ability to deal with anything that might occur. Having politely turned down the initial interview requests, we did agree that he would give one to Sky TV when he arrived in Wales.

The message he gave was simple: this was just another match, he would not assume anything and would referee as best he could whatever came along. It was a calm and measured response and explained his position perfectly: never have preconceived ideas, ever.

He blew the whistle so fast at the first two rucks that it was doubtful the players knew they'd even started, and he kept a tight grip until he felt that things had settled fully. Then he loosened up, and his whole attitude and approach confirmed the very real confidence I had that he was the man for this particular job. Astonishingly, a good match resulted in a draw, 29 points each. Extraordinarily, that meant that only a point had separated the teams over the two matches, despite the ruckus.

The Ref's Call

I am not sure what post-match entertainment Ponty had planned, but Brive were anxious to get out of town fast, which was probably a good idea. As soon as they possibly could, they boarded their coach and headed for the airport.

By a quirk of the then competition rules, it wasn't over yet. These two teams had to meet again in a play-off for the quarter-finals, so it was back to France in early November, Ponty travelling without the three players who were still under French civil judicial investigation.

The referee nomination for the final part of the trilogy would of course be very important, and the tournament organisers were determined that the lid would be kept on things. So the call was made to Jim Fleming, the very well established Scottish international referee. All was peaceful as Brive won, but only by a score, 25–20.

The French team went on to beat Wasps, and then Toulouse, before reaching the final at the neutral venue of Bordeaux. As reigning champions chasing two-in-a-row, they ran into tough opponents, Bath, with Jim Fleming again in charge. Having had a difficult season, Bath played unexpectedly well, and just about pipped the holders. This time the Frenchmen were on the wrong end of a solitary-point victory, 18–19.

Brive felt they were also on the wrong end of a few referee calls, but they missed a couple of kicks which normally would have been nailed, so I didn't think they could complain.

Owen Doyle

But that season is remembered much more for the disastrous events which played out at Le Bar Toulzac at Place des Patriotes-Martyrs.

Chapter Thirteen

10 October 1999

Italy v Tonga in Leicester
(World Cup pool match)

The World Cup has a habit of throwing up unexpected gems, and Tonga against Italy was one of them. The man in the middle was the IRFU's Dave McHugh, and it's 80-plus minutes he will surely never forget.

Intense early Tonga pressure had been rewarded with a half-time lead of 18–12, scoring two tries to none. It was only the boot of the Azzurri's out-half Diego Dominguez keeping them in the hunt.

The second half built in intensity and sheer excitement, as Italy crossed for a converted try of their own, plus another Dominguez penalty, to lead 22–18, and those privileged to be *watching were about to see one of the most extraordinary endgames of any rugby match.*

Tonga would not give up and, following a maul five metres from the Italian line, Isi Fatani barrelled over. The conversion made it 25–22 to the islanders in the 78th minute. It looked all over, only for Dominguez to level things at 25 apiece with yet another penalty as the clock ticked beyond 82 minutes.

Surely, that was it, but with injury time still being played, all eyes were on McHugh and on how much more he would add.

• • •

In the amateur days, the referees would all travel in late July to Clongowes Wood College for a weekend to discuss law interpretation to try and find some sort of consistency. We'd work fairly hard, but never overdid things – certainly there was no fitness test. Then, on the Saturday evening, we would have what could best be termed a bonding session, which involved consuming large quantities of alcohol of any and all description.

Dr Liam Hennessy, who was IRFU director of fitness for 10 years from the year 2000, was undoubtedly one of the very best appointments that the union made; his credentials were long and impressive. An international pole vaulter himself, his work included involvement with Tipperary's

The Ref's Call

All-Ireland senior hurling championship-winning panel, alongside soccer teams Liverpool, Lazio and Bayern Munich. He was also on Pádraig Harrington's backroom team for his three major wins.

Before his arrival, the dogs in the street knew that fitness, or rather the lack of it, was an issue in Irish rugby; everybody will remember the national team playing for about an hour, before fading away to concede late scores and lose matches they might well have won. I shared an office with Hennessy for a while, and we instructed each other in the vagaries of our different roles. I learned a lot more than he did.

The first thing he did was observe the behaviour of the players and look for other reasons for this display of team tiredness. His conclusion was that there were. So, after the next post-match international dinner was over, as the team exited the hotel gates to set off for their normal nocturnal entertainment – nightclub land in Leeson Street – Hennessy was waiting on a parked coach with the doors open. When the players were seated and wondering what was going on, he quietly told them the truth, with no histrionics. If they really wanted to start winning, then the nightclubbing had to cease. It did.

The team bought into this quietly spoken but determined man and Hennessy was in situ for several Triple Crowns and the 2009 Grand Slam.

It was probably well outside his remit, but I asked him if he could find the time to check out the referees' fitness.

Of course he obliged, travelling down to Clongowes one evening and marking out a circuit, several trips around which would amount to three kilometres. Despite the fact that none of our referees had ever done anything similar, Hennessy's view was that information was knowledge so gathering the statistics was a worthwhile exercise. So they set off, and at about the halfway mark I could hardly watch: would they all survive? Future Ireland international Ryan Baird's father Andrew was flying, out in front, but I believe he faded badly and was caught before the end.

I am sure that Baird Snr, a more than reasonable referee, will agree that he was not as good a front-runner as his son is as a player.

The result was that we now knew what had to be done, and Hennessy would play a very important role in getting Irish referees to the high levels of fitness and conditioning needed. Mind you, a few phone calls came in over the next few days after that infamous three-kilometre run, with a number of referees who probably had just a year or two left very wisely deciding to call it a day. This had the added bonus of enabling younger guys to move up through the rankings.

Unfortunately, the 1999 World Cup, the first since the game became fully professional, had come too soon for the changes being made by the referee department to have had a major impact on referee selection for Ireland.

Wales were the main hosts, with the opening match and the final being played in Cardiff, and some other games shared across the rest of the Five Nations countries. It was also the first World Cup where the referees were centrally selected by the International Rugby Board and managed by IRB referee manager Steve Griffiths, who had been appointed to that new role a couple of years earlier. Australia had four referees, and New Zealand and England had three, so it was left to Dave McHugh to be Ireland's sole representative.

As it transpired, Macker would referee a forgotten classic at Leicester's Welford Road, with Tonga and Italy playing out an absolutely pulsating game of rugby. The lead had already changed hands several times when Italian out-half Diego Dominguez nailed a monster penalty to tie the scores 25–25 deep into stoppage time.

With 82 minutes already completed, most assumed that would be that, but McHugh had kept a close eye on his watch and allowed play to continue. Tonga restarted and Italy gathered, but immediately and fatally kicked to touch. Lineout won, Tonga attempted to maul forward but were repelled.

Not giving up and with McHugh visibly warning the Italians to stay onside, Tonga recycled the ball from a ruck and spun it to full-back Sateki Tuipulotu. He was standing in front of the posts but was also only five metres into the Italian half. With barely time to steady himself, he unleashed a monstrous drop kick, and that – the last kick of the match – took the spoils for the Tongans, 28–25.

'The most incredible ending to a rugby match I have ever

seen!' the commentator cried out, and he wasn't wrong. 'The Tongans have gone barmy!' he added. Tuipulotu the hero of the hour with one try, two conversions, two penalties and that drop.

Watching on, my mind went back to eight years previously when Fiji's Opeti Turuva had launched a similar kick during my own World Cup with the whistle, and I was delighted to witness Macker be a part of this one. A game of games, proving, once again, that World Cups are not all about the 'big boys' playing each other.

Ireland's hopes of winning their pool depended on beating Australia at Lansdowne Road. Based on what we had nearly managed in 1991, some were quietly confident that Warren Gatland's men would spring a surprise. But not so; we lost badly, 23–3, meaning we would face Argentina in a play-off for a quarter-final spot.

And so to Lens in the north of France, where having led 21–9, Ireland contrived to lose the last half an hour of play 19–3.

Referee Stuart Dickinson played almost 10 minutes of added time while Ireland battered away continuously at the Argentinian line, including using a 13-man maul tactic, which may not have been the most imaginative use of the ball ever seen. But there was no way through the defence.

Argentina scored the only try of a penalty-riddled match, Gonzalez Quesada and David Humphreys kicking seven each, with 'Humphs' also adding a drop goal, scoring all of Ireland's points, for a final score of 28–24. With the difference being that sole converted try, it was a deflating day for Irish rugby.

The semi-finals produced two epic matches, and really showcased the merits of the tournament. First up was Australia v South Africa at Twickenham, controlled excellently by Welshman Derek Bevan. Locked together on 18 points each, the match went to extra-time, where a 48-metre drop goal by Steve Larkham put Australia ahead, and a late penalty by team-mate Matt Burke sealed the win.

Scotsman Jim Fleming was in charge the following day when France took on New Zealand, who seemed to have things pretty much sown up with a 24–10 lead early in the second half.

But, suddenly, two drop goals and two penalties from Christophe Lamaison brought France back into it. Amazingly, France scored a near-impossible 31 unanswered points, including tries from Dominici, Dourthe and the mercurial Philippe Bernât-Salles. The All Blacks only had the scant last-minute consolation of a converted try, as France romped home 41–31. It was the most amazing turnaround in World Cup history.

France had also topped their pool but had been lucky to do so, helped on their way by an uncharacteristically poor performance from the very highly rated New Zealand referee Paddy O'Brien, in their defeat of Fiji.

Fiji were denied what looked to everyone a perfect try, but the whistle blew for a French scrum, a knock-on according to O'Brien. There then followed several other dubious calls, all going against the islanders – France were awarded a doubtful penalty try, and another came from a move which appeared to contain a few forward passes.

It could have been the end of a top-class referee, but O'Brien faced into the storm and took this performance on the chin. It was a tough road back, but he showed character and determination to overcome such a massive blow; others may well have walked away. It was a considerable achievement to 'get back on the horse'.

The final was refereed by South Africa's André Watson, but did not live up to the quality of the semis. As in 1987, France failed to find their mojo in consecutive matches, scoring only four penalties from the boot of Christophe Lamaison, with Australia winning 35–12, becoming the first team to win the Webb Ellis Cup twice.

We stuck to Clongowes as our annual conference venue for a few years, but the format was now very different. It was professionally structured, and was the main driver in delivering consistency across all the provinces at all levels. The same messages would then be conveyed by the development managers in each province across the various levels of referee development.

We also introduced tests on the laws of the game, which were very revealing. Any budding referee who opens the law book will be immediately struck by its complexity and detail; it is nearly impossible to get to know it all. Despite many attempts over the years to simplify matters, it still has 21 laws; and while that doesn't sound too bad, all of them have many subsections. And then there are important definitions to get to know as well – so instead of 21 pages, there are 164.

The moral of that story is that all the detail must be known inside out, the impact of not knowing every dot and comma is all too capable of changing a result. Mind you, a referee would need to be Archimedes to understand the laws around replacements, substitutions and uncontested scrums – it is a veritable nightmare.

So some referees' knowledge was poor, but this built up over a few seasons, and detailed law knowledge remained a high priority. To my amazement, Olan Trevor, then a regular interpro referee, failed miserably; it turned out that he had actually got them all correct, but when he heard that Dave McHugh had set the paper, he changed most of his answers, convinced that 'trick' questions had been in the mix.

The referees themselves were aghast that their knowledge was not at the level they had thought. The laws of the game are complicated and need careful study – not just knowing them by rote learning but understanding them inside out, and the reasons for the detailed minutiae.

Armed with such complete knowledge, a referee is much more likely to deliver a sound performance when the going gets tough, and not be surprised when something out of the ordinary happens.

Fitness levels were based on the requirements of the

elite end of the game, and the notorious beep test was introduced. The level of testing was decided by the referees themselves, who chose to challenge themselves to the maximum, and always followed the IRB standard for international refs. This was commendable indeed as most would be operating in the All Ireland League and no higher. The test also proved a great source of camaraderie, with referees egging each other on to see who would be the last man standing. We eventually had to set a maximum limit on proceedings to ensure they didn't push themselves too hard, which actually had started to happen.

If I had to pick one development tool that was worth its weight in gold to us, it would be the introduction of the referee camera. Video expert Peter Beamish was employed to wire up referees for sound, then film their performances, with the ref never to be out of the picture. This meant that we, and the ref, could watch back his positioning and his accuracy of decision-making, and hear his interaction with the players. One referee did not believe me when I phoned to tell him that a CD was in the post, and could he please listen to his level of shouting at the players as it really wasn't acceptable. The recording told no lies. His disbelief quickly turned to utter astonishment and it proved to be a great learning experience for him. His wife overheard the video and advised him that if she was ever spoken to like that, he'd be packing a little suitcase and leaving, never to return.

In an effort to leave no stone unturned, we also

introduced sports psychology, through the very able Dr Tadhg MacIntyre, which was a definite and innovative addition to the programme. Individuals who availed of it inevitably found it to be more than useful.

When the top men and women in our pool of referees started to get more and more elite appointments, the buzz and the motivation was extraordinary. We probably turned over that top 50 list of referees at least six times during my tenure, and I can safely say that every one of them is entitled to a share of the elite programme success. We all owned it.

Chapter Fourteen

17 January 1998

*Llanharan v Tondu in Llanharan Dairy Field
(Second XV Junior League derby match)*

*The match was reaching its conclusion, on what has been a
wet and muddy afternoon.*

*In injury-time, referee David Evans reset what was
probably to be the last scrum. However, the front rows did not
engage properly and the whistle was blown for another reset.*

*But Richard Vowles, the Llanharan hooker, had fallen to
the ground. A hush fell over those in attendance as the
seriousness of the situation beaome apparent.*

*The moment would cause reverberations around the rugby
world and have a terrible effect on Vowles' life.*

• • •

The Ref's Call

In 2001, and in situ as the IRFU's director of referees, I received a phone call from Winifred Wilson-Williams at Morgan Cole, solicitors for St Paul's Insurance Company. Wilson-Williams wanted to discuss a case taken by a Welsh amateur player, Richard Vowles, who had suffered catastrophic spinal injuries while playing for his club Llanharan's Second XV.

Not unsurprisingly, Vowles and his advisors had taken a case against the referee David Evans, the Welsh Rugby Union and coaches involved in the match. In all, there were seven defendants, with Evans being the 'first defendant'.

Through my contacts in the WRU, I had heard about the awful incident but I had never formally discussed it with anyone. The question put to me was whether or not I would be prepared to act as an expert witness in the case. I replied that I would consider it, but that I would not act 'for' them or argue their case. If I found evidence that the referee was in the wrong, then that would have to be said. Now, that position suited the UK system – both sides appoint an expert witness who supplies his or her determination to the court, and then discuss their findings together and see what common ground there is.

I was somewhat reluctant, but having discussed it with our CEO Philip Browne, I knew that it was necessary to front up and assist this case in any way I could. I didn't know the extent of my involvement then, and neither did I know what a worrying workload it would turn out to be. When the case papers and witness statements were delivered, the huge importance of it all became clear. This would not be a quick opinion, and it required many nights and weekends of long reading, many walks on the beach to consider everything in the various statements to start to form my view.

The referee involved, David Evans was a solicitor and had a strong record of looking after players' safety. In one instance, he had been roundly criticised for refusing to start a match because there was no padding for the posts, but he had stood his ground firmly. That was impressive but for me it could have no bearing on this one tragic incident.

The circumstances of the injury were quite involved. After about 30 minutes, the Llanharan loose-head prop Gavin Marsh got injured; he could not continue and they did not have cover available on the bench. The referee offered the option to Llanharan of uncontested scrums, but as the regulation stated that a side which caused non-contested scrums would forfeit the valuable league points, that offer was not taken up. The other option, which was fully allowed and covered in the laws of the game at that point in time – was that if Llanharan had another player who could play in that position, he could be tried out there and then the match could continue with normal scrums. They elected to play their wing-forward Chris Jones as a suitable replacement for Marsh, and the match continued. Jones was in that position for about an hour before that fateful scrum.

The atrocious conditions on the day contributed to more

than the usual number of resets, and that continued after the introduction of Jones to the front row. I researched matches at the same level played in Ireland under similar conditions, and by then our referee assessors had been instructed to count both the number of scrums, and the number of collapses. What I read in those assessments was not perception, but rather fact. Adding in an error tolerance, it was clear that there were many collapses in such weather conditions.

Bit by bit, I started to wonder what, if anything, the referee could or should have done differently. He had offered uncontested scrums, and he had allowed Jones to go into the front row, a decision that was not his, but the team's.

With my outline opinion that this had been a tragic accident, I went to the chambers of John Leighton Williams QC, at Farrar's Buildings, Temple, London. There, in the land of Horace Rumpole, he and his team, very politely and at length, interrogated my views fully, and felt that they would stand the test of cross-examination. In fact, they had been so polite, that before I left I asked them to pose some difficult questions that might come from such a cross-examination. The reply was, 'But we have just asked you those.'

The conclusion of all of this was that the WRU would defend the allegations of negligence and that the trial would proceed. The WRU were genuinely concerned that a ruling in favour of the claimant would have a very serious negative effect on the participation of referees across all levels of the amateur game. And so, in December 2002, we all departed for the High Court in Cardiff, where the case was heard by Mr Justice Morland. There was no jury.

Mr Leighton Williams argued the case for David Evans very well, and he also included in his argument that a referee in an amateur game could not be expected to have the same duty of care as existed in the professional game. I was grilled by Mr Ian Murphy QC and stood firmly by my conclusion that this had been an accident. But below the surface, I found it very hard not to feel that some sort of 'without prejudice' settlement could be reached.

Obviously, I had spoken to Evans, who I found to be a highly respectable and straightforward man; and I also met Richard Vowles during the trial, a fine young man, facing his injury with absolute courage and dignity. There was also a dreadful irony to the events of that day: Richard Vowles had expected to be reserve and not to be playing. It was only because his brother had been called up to the first team that Richard took his place at hooker for the seconds.

At the conclusion of the trial, the general feeling seemed to be that the prosecution had not done enough to establish negligence. But the overriding thought was: 'never second guess a judge'. Justice Morland had worked assiduously throughout, making copious notes, intervening rarely but, when he did, it was with unexpected but highly relevant questions. His attention never wavered.

The Ref's Call

He informed the court that he would take some weeks to finalise his judgment, as he had to depart for the town of Mold where he was due to oversee a murder trial. But he still had time to invite the two leading counsel to his rooms for lunch before concluding the trial.

Some weeks later, when Justice Morland, sitting in London's High Court, delivered his verdict, it both surprised and worried all referees. The written word of it ran to 20 pages.

Early in the judgment, it was confirmed that the second defendants, the WRU, accepted vicarious liability for the first defendant, David Evans. In other words, in the event of the claimant being successful, then the WRU would accept responsibility for Evans' actions and the financial costs involved. But, it must be added, no referee wants to be held in any way responsible for such a catastrophic injury. During the trial, it was clear that the whole event was taking a toll on Evans.

Justice Morland went on to state that, while the witness statements were taken some two years after the match, which itself had taken place over four years previously, there was little doubt as to the general picture of what happened during the game.

The learned judge went on to outline the dreadful weather conditions on the day of the game, that it was a hard-fought match but not dirty, and that there were many set scrums. He talked about Christopher Jones, the replacement prop, who had never been trained as a front-row forward but had played there occasionally some years earlier in low-level games.

He then addressed the duty of care issue: 'Mr Leighton Williams boldly submitted that I should hold that, as a matter of policy, no such duty exists,' he said. At the trial, I'd thought that the judge had winced slightly at this submission by the Queen's Counsel, but that maybe I'd imagined it. But here were the words of the judge now confirming with absolute clarity that there did indeed exist such a duty.

His Lordship stated that he did not consider it logical that a line should be drawn between the amateur and professional games, and that the risk of very serious injury in the amateur was more likely to occur than in the professional game, although such occurrences were extremely infrequent.

His judgment went on to say that as a matter of policy it is 'fair, just and reasonable' that the law should impose upon an amateur referee of an amateur rugby match a duty of care towards the safety of the players.

It then quoted the then relevant law of rugby which allowed Jones to move from the back row into the position of prop. *In the event of a front-row player ordered off or injured, or both, the referee, in the interests of safety, will confer with the captain of his team whether another player is suitably trained/ experienced to take his position.* This permitted a player to be tried in the front row, rather than having uncontested scrums.

In practice, a referee would accept the nomination of

such a player and would not cross-examine him as to his front-row training or his suitability for the position of loose-head prop.

Despite the fact that most witness statements were made about two years after the match, Justice Morland commented on how the evidence of David Evans, whom he found to be 'an impressive and accurate witness', was the exception, being based on notes he made immediately following events. Evans' oral evidence was absolutely consistent with both his match pad entry and his referee's report.

Finally, to sum up the crux of the judgment, the major points of Justice Morland's verdict were:

- That David Evans was not negligent in his handling of the set scrums or of the match in general. But that he did abdicate his responsibility in leaving it to Llanharan to decide not to have non-contested scrums, and that he made no enquiries of Christopher Jones as to whether or not he had the necessary, suitably trained experience. The judge stated that the decision was taken at a stoppage in play, but that there had been no interrogation of Jones.

- The judge did not accept Christopher Jones' description of the accident but stated that both teams were crouched down and that it occurred because of a mistiming of the engagement, which had been the suggested reason in my submission. Further, that Evans should have kept the trialling of Jones in the front row under constant review; and that he should have ordered uncontested scrums before the accident, given the increasing number of collapses. This would have been a very tall order for any referee in the heat of a hard and closely fought game; in the written word it seemed a very reasonable point of view.

- Jones' recollection, though, was undoubtedly honest and as he remembered it. His recall was that Llanharan were not yet in the crouch position, but that simply confirms the problems faced with all participants' or witnesses' statements to any accident; six statements, for example, may provide a number of different accounts as to what happened.

The verdict really came down to the judge deciding that Evans had breached his duty of care and that had been a material cause of the accident; and that Jones' lack of technique as a prop was a significant contributory cause of the many collapses and of the mistimed engagement.

There were some who felt that the judge had seen, on the one hand, an incapacitated young man, wheelchair-bound and, on the other, the WRU and a large insurance company, and that he had bent over backwards to ensure that Vowles would receive compensation. I do not really hold with that, having thought about it often enough over the years. My belief is that the judge was absolutely correct

Peter Stringer sets up an attack for Munster
under the watchful eye of Alan Lewis, August 2008

Post his international career, Donal Courtney made a massive contribution to the appointment system for referees, May 2010

The ever-genial Alan Lewis chats with English coach Martin Johnson, February 2009

Challenge Cup final, Toulon v Cardiff, May 2010
Alain Rolland leads a full team of Irish officials (Kevin Beggs and
Alan Rogan joining the international trio of Rolland, Lewis and Clancy)

Wales v France, Rugby World Cup semi-final, October 2011,
Alain Rolland dismisses Sam Warburton; it will never be forgotten

Ireland v Wales, Six Nations Championship, February 2013, long before Joy Neville thought of whistling, she had an international career that spanned 10 years, below she takes a lineout catch during Ireland's 2013 Grand Slam campaign

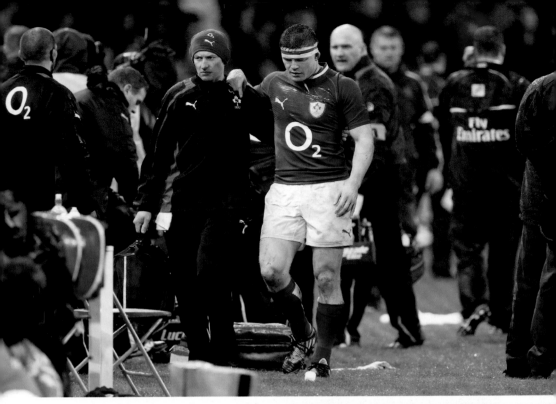

Above: Brian O'Driscoll is assisted off the field, Ireland v France, March 2013

Right: Peter Fitzgibbon and Bundee Aki enjoy a cosy chat, December 2015

Above: Johnny Lacey,
Heineken Cup try
scorer and international
referee – a rare breed;
February 2017

Left: Joy Neville,
Ulster v Southern
Kings, February 2018

In 2015, Helen O'Reilly became the first woman to referee in the All Ireland League. She's pictured here at the Women's All Ireland League Division 1 final at Energia Park, Donnybrook, April 2019

George Clancy, January 2020, the young hurler from Bruff who became an international rugby referee

on the duty-of-care issue, and then applied very clear reasoning to the laws of rugby that existed then. Would a different judge have reached a different conclusion? We will, of course, never know.

David Evans and his family were terribly upset by the events. He did not believe that the outcome – to blame him – was fair and reasonable, and many agreed. Other defendants included the Llanharan coaches, who were found not culpable. Though it's difficult to imagine that they would not have known Jones' capabilities and the wisdom of playing him in the front row. It is also difficult to imagine them disputing the ref's decision, which would have appeared a normal call to them.

When the verdict was declared, the IRFU immediately stopped the practice of allowing players to be trialled in the front row. Either there were suitably trained front-row players on the bench or there were not; and, if not, it was to be uncontested scrums forthwith. Teams would not forfeit league points if they could not remain with contested scrums, rather each case would be judged on its own merits. Referees in Ireland were reassured by that immediate action. They also got much-needed confirmation that the IRFU was fully insured in the event of any referee being sued and that vicarious liability was accepted.

The IRFU also held numerous scrum clinics that were obligatory for anyone who refereed matches at any level, whether official referees or those who reffed occasionally, for example a team coach. The attendances were huge.

But the WRU weren't finished and took the case to the Court of Appeal, which was heard in London some months later. Despite the stringent arguments of Leighton Williams QC, the court upheld the trial verdict; and, finally, the House of Lords refused to hear the case. The verdict stood.

It's very hard to take any positives from such a catastrophic injury, but in actuality some good did come from it. Justice Morland's judgment ensured that the scrummage laws were fully reviewed, and the law to try out a player in the front row was removed from the game. In future, the front-row positions in the scrum would only be filled by players whose normal role was prop or hooker; effectively, they would become specialist players. Also introduced were new engagement procedures that reduced very much the potential for mistiming. This all meant that the chances of a catastrophic front-row injury were very much diminished and the game would be much safer.

But mainly, of course, Richard Vowles received a level of compensation that would go some way towards helping him to live a normal life, though nothing could give him back what he had lost on that terrible day.

Chapter Fifteen

December 1995

*IRFU referee committee meeting at
the Berkley Court Hotel in Ballsbridge*

'We've two matches, France v England and Wales v France,'
said the referee committee chair Malcolm Little. 'So, we have
to appoint two referees from our three-man panel, that's Dave
McHugh, Brian Stirling and Alan Lewis. Who'd like to speak
first?'

Once again, the debate went on long into the night,
continuing over a pleasant dinner. The committee always
liked to reach a consensus but there were strongly held
views within the group and it always took a lot of
discussion.

My doubts that this process was really fit for purpose

were steadily growing, but as yet there was no evident alternative.

• • •

When I took over the IRFU role, I really disliked the process involved in selecting the referees for the Five Nations and other Test matches.

It was within the IRFU referee committee's remit to make these appointments and, inevitably, there was quite a bit of subjectivity involved. The committee tried very hard to be fair and to consider merit as much as it could before finalising its choices, but where there's subjectivity, personal preferences invariably also came into play. Also, three into two never works, and it was with much reluctance that someone had to be left out.

It was a system that I could not see surviving in the new age of professionalism.

So I had been delighted when, in 1997, the International Rugby Board took over the job of making these calls under a centralised merit-based system, following the appointment of the first IRB referee manager, Steve Griffiths, and three selectors, Peter Brook, David Burnett and Dick Byers. At that point, we were stealing a march on other unions with our development and coaching programme, and I was sure that if we produced the quality, then our referees would be picked on merit. The theory was that this would mean we'd get more Test matches, not fewer, which is exactly how things turned out.

In fact, we had many who would have been eligible, but the competition was really stiff. Simon McDowell, another Ulsterman, must have reffed just about everything going and went to several World Cups as an assistant or TMO. But that final step to full international status just, frustratingly, eluded him.

Marshall (now there's a name for a referee) Kilgore had a lovely touch, but he never really reached the level of fitness necessary to enable him to challenge for serious representative honours.

Munster's Olan Trevor was another very fine ref. Quietly firm, he brought a lot to the table, but, again, the competition was in the way. There were many others who performed in the Celtic League or in Europe, and they too can be proud of their achievements. What each and every one contributed was of great value. They were all true team players, and when acting as assistants always went the extra mile in that role.

The introduction of the European Cup had been followed by the formation of the Celtic League in 2001 but that brought very particular and unwelcome problems.

The main issue was that Ireland had serious numbers capable of refereeing at that level, whereas some other unions did not. But they wanted equality of opportunity in terms of the number of matches allocated to each union. My position was that an overall panel should be picked, and each referee then be given an equal number of matches, provided, of course, that there were no train crashes on the way. That seemed the fairest way to go and also it would drive quality rather than quantity. It would also mean that merit not neutrality would prevail. That was what was happening in the southern hemisphere's Super Rugby, which had for a long time favoured the merit-based approach.

There was massive difficulty in getting this accepted, but eventually it went through. For Irish referees, it meant that everyone who deserved a chance got it. Then of course, they had to perform.

However, it remained a severe bone of contention, and another solution had to be found. Step forward 1995 World Cup final referee Ed Morrison, who was approached and agreed to take over the appointments for all matches in the Celtic League. He had previously been the England elite referee manager, so knew his way around the block; it was ideal. He was also the point of contact for the coaches, who could now make their views known, and that gave some serious additional information to assist him in the role.

By the time the 2003 World Cup rolled around, we'd doubled our representation, with Dave McHugh and Alain Rolland travelling to Australia as Ireland's referees, alongside Alan Lewis and Donal Courtney as touch judges. The first three had reffed in that year's Six Nations and I'd had high hopes that they'd all go as referees, they really deserved it.

The Ref's Call

In the heel of the hunt, Lewis did get to referee, as a pre-tournament injury to Australia's Scott Young meant a replacement was required.

For McHugh, it was a nice contrast to 12 months previously, when he'd been the victim of a cowardly attack during a South Africa v New Zealand game in Durban. He had just indicated an All Blacks' scrum, when a drunken South African fan named Pieter Van Zyl ran onto the pitch. His sole intent was to assault the referee, which he duly did, dragging McHugh to the ground and dislocating his shoulder. Opposing players, particularly Richie McCaw and A.J. Venter, joined forces to prevent this outcome from being a lot worse, and, believe me, it might well have been. But Macker being Macker, he was back on the proverbial horse as soon as his injury healed and a World Cup spot was the least he deserved.

Once again, Australia had four referees initially selected, all good men, but none of them figured in the knockout stages. So I believe I can rest my case that we might well have had at least one more in the original selection.

Rolland was in the middle for England's 28–17 quarter-final win over Wales, an extraordinary bullet-train-like rise to such eminence since he'd only started to referee four years earlier. That said, I can personally vouch for the fact that he'd pretty much 'refereed' all his matches as a top (and Ireland-capped) scrum-half! Poacher turned game-keeper extraordinaire.

Referee fitness and conditioning were, rightly, high on

the agenda of IRB referee manager Steve Griffiths, as they should have been; and everyone knew there would be testing when they arrived in Australia. But in the view of many it's not a good idea to test during a tournament. After all, you've picked your team and the refs have already been slotted into their pool matches. So why not just get on with it?

There is also the risk of injury, which is exactly what happened. The facilities for the sprint test were undoubtedly not fit for purpose; it was a small school gym and not long enough to carry out the required distance, so it was decided to run more or less diagonally, which just about provided enough space. However, the runoff, or slowing-down space, was extremely limited, and the referees had to take a hard turn off the timber flooring onto concrete, avoid a soft-drinks machine and pull up sharply.

Later on, these three factors were blamed for the injuries, of varying seriousness, to five officials: Donal Courtney, Joël Dumé, Bryce Lawrence, Scott Young and Nigel Whitehouse.

In fact, Young damaged his calf so badly that he could take no further part in the tournament, and as a consequence never refereed at a World Cup.

Rumours were flying around that several referees had failed their fitness test and that some would be sent home. The chairman of the IRB, former IRFU stalwart Syd Millar, vented his annoyance at this state of affairs and referee manager Steve Griffiths came under significant pressure to fix the problem.

While those who were injured would be tested later, Griffiths moved quickly to reschedule tests for those not hurt and the results were positive; all passed.

This included Peter Marshall, who had been allocated the key South Africa v England match, which he did very well indeed, without once breaking into a sprint, as was his casual wont.

Another casualty was Frenchman Joël Dumé, who had travelled as an assistant and was at the end of his career. Having been injured, his re-test could only be scheduled after he had sufficiently recovered to officiate in his first match. However, he then failed the re-test, and was told he was being withdrawn, a decision I've always found to have been extremely insensitive and unnecessary. Dumé had served the game very well over a long career and deserved far better treatment.

The more sensible system of referees being tested before competitions, and not at them, came into place shortly afterwards; it was long overdue.

This was the first World Cup that saw the introduction of bonus points and the TMO, a technological advance that would change the game forever by taking elements of decision-making off the pitch and into a studio.

The intention had been that New Zealand and Australia would share the tournament; but a contractual dispute over stadium advertising rights between the New Zealand Rugby Football Union and Rugby World Cup saw all matches being moved to Australia.

The last moments of the final when Australia met England in Sydney will be the stuff of debate for generations. Leading with three minutes left, England knocked on and André Watson blew for an Australian scrum; it collapsed and was reset. England captain Martin Johnson had voiced his view to the referee that Australia should be pinged; Watson quite rightly ignored him. The reset scrum went down again, and this time Watson penalised England, with little hesitation. It seemed a very harsh call, but one that the referee has always stoutly defended, despite the fact that England's had been the dominant scrum during the match. Elton Flately, with typical insouciance, levelled the scores at 14 each.

And so to extra-time, where one penalty each had brought the scores to 17–17. Less than a minute remained, and a sudden-death finish in the form of a drop goal shootout was looming, an appalling way to decide the game. Then, came some marvellous English skillsets, precisely delivered and often forgotten in the euphoria of the actual winning kick.

On the right-hand touchline, England bravely went long to the tail of the lineout, a wonderful throw by Steve Thompson. Fast ball off the top from Lewis Moody saw the backs get onto serious front-foot rugby. With the defence expecting a pass back to Jonny Wilkinson, Matt Dawson instead sniped down the side of the ruck, gaining more, very valuable yardage to bring play deep into the Aussie 22. Another ruck, this time Dawson does pass to Wilkinson. Off his weaker right foot and under remarkable pressure but with ice in his veins, he slotted the drop goal of his life, and the Webb Ellis Cup was on its way to England. The drop goal is remembered and Wilkinson as the hero, but it had been a wonderful collective team effort; Dawson had handled three times and the ball had gone through a total of 10 English hands, not a single error in a moment of peak pressure. Rugby at its finest.

All of England was incensed at the scrum decision, and Wilkinson's winning kick, from the point of view of the match officials group and also that of the IRB, was probably a damn good thing. One still shudders to think of the levels of abuse that would have been hurled at Watson had England lost. It was Watson's second final, and he remains the only referee to have two under his belt, which is quite some achievement.

It's always a fun exercise to try and guess the referees for the knockout stages, especially for the final, and many, myself included, considered that this time around Paddy O'Brien deserved the honour.

Once more, Ireland met their regular foes from South America, just pipping Argentina 16–15 in the pool stages, scoring the only try of the match through Alan Quinlan, and so qualified to meet France in the quarter-final. In that match, France led 27–0 at half-time, including three converted tries. The final score was 43–21, and that did not flatter a very strong, pacey French team, captained by Fabien Galthié, who became their national coach in 2019.

That annoying habit Ireland had of being unable to make it past the quarters continued.

As McHugh's active career was entering its final quarter, I suggested he might like to do some development work. To his reasonable question of 'How much?' I replied that there'd be no extra money, but that if we designated a portion of his current income to development and increased that percentage over time, when he'd finished blowing the whistle he'd still have a role in the organisation.

Having bought into that idea, it's fair to say he worked his socks off, becoming a most valued employee, and a top-class referee coach. He travelled the length and breadth of the four provinces, searching out talent and giving development courses. Perhaps a little unexpectedly, he became really good at it, and passionate about performance improvement.

As a result of the reputation Macker had built, Clive Woodward came calling. The England World Cup-winning coach had been appointed as head coach of the Lions for their 2005 tour, their first visit to New Zealand since 1993. He was preparing assiduously for the assault on the All Black citadel, determined to leave no stone unturned.

In an effort to keep the number of penalties conceded at

a low number, and to ensure that he had the right law knowledge to hand, he called up Macker. While Woodward could have turned to a fellow countryman, he knew that here was a man whose law knowledge and game understanding was pretty much unmatched. It was a great honour and the IRFU were more than happy to release him for the tour.

While improvements at international level had now been embedded, the same old problems around appointments had developed in the European competitions, the Heineken and Challenge cups. Because there was no referee manager, there was nothing coming through from the clubs, and certain referees were being promoted and then appointed on the basis of anecdotal comments. It was terribly frustrating.

Former Ireland international Derek McGrath had been appointed as CEO of the ERC, who ran these tournaments. He was to prove a top-class appointment, more than ably supported by his PA, Sarah Nelson, who contributed enormously to the smooth running of the organisation. McGrath also knew and understood the importance of quality match officials, and that they could have an enormous impact on the standard of the rugby on offer. He formed what was known as the match officials subcommittee, which was responsible for advising on the form of their referees and then allocating the appointments. He always made a point of being present at group meetings unless it was really impossible. So too did ERC

Chairman Jean-Pierre Lux, further underlining the board's interest in the processes around officiating, and that it was a priority for them.

After one extraordinarily tense meeting in Dublin's Shelbourne Hotel, McGrath approached me. Did I think that a full-time referee manager should be appointed, and would I chair a small group to see if, how and when this should be done? He had obviously noticed that I had nearly blown a fuse at the meeting and had left the room to re-trip the switch. The problems centred around my belief that a number of Scottish and Italian referees were not measuring up, a view unsurprisingly not shared by their representatives, so discussion had, inevitably, become fraught. And again, the problem of anecdotal opinion, rather than evidence-based information, raised its ugly head.

The small group got together and it didn't take long to decide that things could not continue as they were, my fuse box wouldn't be able to cope. Very shortly afterwards, an advertisement appeared and the position was launched. Having advised McGrath that the role of referee manager was agreed by my group, good business practice decreed that I would have no involvement on the interview panel, who ended up very interested in an application from former Irish international referee Donal Courtney. After several chats with him, the appointment was eventually made in May 2009 and it proved an inspired choice. Steeped in business governance, Courtney brought a very well-reasoned clarity to the job and proposed appointments without fear or favour, presenting meticulously researched, evidence-based reasoning for his choices.

The match officials subcommittee would then sit around the table and listen to his rationale for the many selections he had to make for each weekend's matches and for the critical knockout stages. Courtney backed up his choices with real evidence, from the referee performance reviewers and from the team coaches; video clips of crucial errors were also reviewed. It was all pretty watertight – the arguments not only dissipated, they disappeared. He was in the role until 2016, and if the subcommittee changed even a handful of appointments in that time, then that was about it.

The circle was squared fully with Courtney sitting on the IRB referee selection panel, as did his southern hemisphere counterpart Lyndon Bray. That meant a steady flow of accurate information, enabling the best performers from both hemispheres to get through to the top.

The subjectivity of the early days was long gone at that point, and the world was working together to find the best international referees. Perfect? Maybe not, but how very much better than before.

As time went by, it was clear that help was needed at both the elite and domestic game levels. Bit by bit, the union released more money and it became possible to employ referee development personnel in each province – though, very importantly, they were employed by the union, and reported to me. All of them refereed to at least Pro14 level, which meant an abundance of talent working in the department, and all but one remained in situ after my departure, although in varying roles. First in the door was Clongowes College 'old boy' David Keane, a very good referee in the seven-a-side game, with over a hundred World Rugby Sevens Series matches to his credit. His initial responsibility was running a schoolboy refereeing scheme, aided and abetted by volunteer Gerry Maher, a teacher in Roscrea College.

International referee and fluent French speaker Peter Fitzgibbon came in later from the then-termed leisure rugby section, and Keane went over to a role in that department. David Wilkinson, subsequently appointed national referee manager a few years ago, also joined the team, with Ulster his responsibility. And when his professional refereeing career was over in 2021, Sean Gallagher took up his old role in Leinster. David O'Brien is the odd man out, as he left the union, just a bit earlier than me, to return to third-level studies. Together with Dave McHugh, this was a very knowledgeable, enthusiastic, hard-working group, as good as any in the world in terms of development.

There had also been a very important appointment that helped the process. Former Leinster player Eddie Wigglesworth, who had been working as rugby chief in Leinster, replaced the affable New Zealander Ray Southam as the IRFU's director of rugby. Southam had left things in good shape and Wigglesworth can be more than happy with his own legacy; crucially, he recognised the importance of refereeing, despite the fact it cost money and was never going to earn any.

We did several very good things together, including pushing through the under-19 law scrum variations to the lower levels of adult rugby. This was done for player safety reasons but was still vehemently opposed by some people who should have known better. That opposition was thwarted by the formation of an expert group who agreed, and decided, that player safety must come first.

Chapter Sixteen

20 May 2007

Leicester Tigers v Wasps in Twickenham
(Heineken Cup final)

The match was just seven minutes old when, in front of a baying, record crowd of 81,076, Lewie brought all his savoir-faire to bear. Did Wasps' captain Lawrence Dallaglio deserve a yellow card after being caught on the wrong side of the tackle area?

'No' is the answer, but he did need a clear message and he got it, accompanied by a penalty.

'You've been muttering at me since the start. Now, anything else from you and I know you know the result. It'll be a card, the colour to be decided.'

I nodded approvingly. It was exactly what was needed.

The Ref's Call

There wasn't another issue in a match where a first-half try from Wasps' former Munster scrum-half Eoin Reddan set them on their way to victory.

Despite none of our teams being involved, it was a good day for the Irish at Twickenham.

• • •

When we first got cracking on aiming to become the best of the best, Dave McHugh was the foundation stone and his career at the top had already started. The first thing was the identification of upcoming talent to ensure there would be contenders to join him and, eventually, to take over when he hung up his whistle in 2004. Succession planning was key to everything we did, as was our determination to never rest on our laurels; it was important to be hungry for more. The men and women who followed were at the centre of what transpired to be a golden age.

Alan Lewis is perhaps the most interesting case study of elite referee development, and what is needed to both maximise talent and ensure consistent, coherent performances at the highest level of rugby.

When I first came across Lewie, he was a swashbuckling cricketer. An instinctive batsman with great touch and feel, he would swipe runs to all corners wherever he played, and wasn't averse to showing his unhappiness when a close lbw decision went against him and he had to depart the crease early. He followed his father Ian onto the international stage, just as Alan's own daughters Gaby and Robyn have done. No less than a sporting dynasty.

That touch and feel approach was central to his success as a referee, but it did not come easy and was not without its trials and tribulations. His natural instinct for the game was overshadowed by the lack of structure he brought to his refereeing when he first started out.

In many ways, this is easy to understand; it had all come very easily to him in cricket and he had climbed quickly through the refereeing ranks too.

The first sign of something being not quite right was a Barbarians match, when he decided that he'd join in the fun. Basically, it was a case of anything and everything being allowed by the referee. Sure, the Baa-Baas' ethos is to play open, attractive rugby but, nonetheless, they play hardball when opponents are allowed to slow the ball or close down space. Their matches are not easy assignments, and this one certainly turned out to be extremely tricky.

His first major international assignment was as touch judge for Scotland v South Africa in 1994, my last international, and I'm delighted to be able to say we shared a match together.

A debut with the whistle came a few years later when Australia played Fiji, and then he got a very big slice of luck in the 2001 Six Nations. Driving to Dublin Airport for a flight to Paris to be assistant to Dave McHugh for the

France v Wales clash, word came through that Macker had been taken ill and could not make the trip. So, without weeks of preparation and worry, Lewie jumped in at the deep end. It was a scintillating match as Wales came out on top by 43–35.

His performance reviewer was the eminent French rugby man Michel Lamoulie, whose glowing report held a huge amount of sway where it mattered.

But while things were going well, there was still the capacity for Lewie to have a sudden dip in performance, and, in the European Cup, his reputation was suffering. He was finding it hard to get a grip of things and, as a result, his career was stuttering. He came to see me. 'I need help here,' he said, so we chatted for an hour or so. It was clear that he had many wires crossed in his thinking, and it was having a massively negative impact on his planning and preparation for top matches.

First stop, I thought, was to get an expert to untangle his thoughts, so I pointed him in the direction of sports psychologist Tom Moriarty. He, very effectively, did the necessary business and that left Lewie and myself with a clear whiteboard to get on with the rugby end of things.

The net result of many, many hours' work over the summer of 2004 was a clear plan for each specific game area, how he would deal with problematic issues and how he would communicate with players. None of this was designed to curb his natural flair and affability, both very strong points. It was not an easy task, but he mastered it completely, with the very positive results now part of refereeing history.

Colin High was the English elite referee manager at the time. A straight-talking former international ref, he had been very concerned at some of Lewie's performances. He went to see him refereeing the Leicester v Biarritz Heineken Cup tie a few months after our summer work, about which we had said nothing. Shortly after the match my phone rang. It was High. 'I just watched someone who looked very like Lewie, but is a completely different referee. Don't know what you guys have been up to, but it's worked, he is going to go far.' A more honest appraisal, typical of the very likeable High, you could not get.

And he was absolutely right. Lewie went right to the top, and became one of the most popular referees of his generation.

Along the way, there were many highlights, including South Africa v France at Kings Park, Durban, in 2005. An epic clash, it ended in a seesawing 30–30 draw.

In New Zealand, he'll be remembered for handing out three yellow cards to the All Blacks against England at Twickenham in 2005. Perhaps, some thought, he might have held off on the last one, but each offence deserved the sanction. Coach Graham Henry was not pleased, naturally enough, and would later remark that his team hadn't received three yellow cards over the course of many previous matches, and here they got them all in one go. Nevertheless, despite playing with 14 men for most of the second-half, Henry's team held on for a 23–19 win, another terrific match.

While Lewie did referee in the 2003 World Cup, he was originally selected as a touch judge, but by 2011, he was omitted from the travelling party altogether. Both were quirks of selection, which might well have gone his way, particularly 2003. In the 2007 quarter-final, Fiji gave South Africa one heck of a fright, pulling back to level at 20–20, before the Springboks saved their bacon with a late try and penalty. Lewie's performance in that match put the earlier disappointment of his original selection as an assistant in 2003 firmly in the shade.

The European Cup final of 2007 saw two English teams, Wasps and Leicester, battle it out in front of a record crowd. It was a fairly open secret that both sides got the referee they wished for, our own Alan Lewis.

It was an absolute classic, with Wasps turning the tables on Leicester, who were firm favourites to complete a historic three-in-a-row. Without a doubt it was one of Lewie's finest matches, and I was able to sit in the stand and just enjoy the spectacle, not one moment of concern.

Chapter Seventeen

8 October 2007

*Alain Rolland announced as referee
for the Rugby World Cup final in Paris*

*The Left Bank Montparnasse area has got to be the best
arrondissement in Paris. I love it.*

*Not far from Luxembourg Gardens, La Sorbonne,
St-Germain-des-Prés and the Seine, it has restaurants and
cafés of pretty much every cuisine and price. Throw in the
wonderful food markets on the boulevards of Édouard Quintet
and Raspail, with an artisan bakery across the road, and
there were plenty of worse places to base oneself for a World
Cup.*

*That night in the La Rotonde brasserie, it felt like all the
work of the previous 12 years had been worthwhile.*

The Ref's Call

We toasted the first Irishman to be appointed to take charge of the biggest game in world rugby. Lewis and I happily quaffed champagne bubbles. Rolland of course quaffed – ahem – water.

Did I enjoy having a hand in it and bathing in the reflected glory of a fantastic achievement? You bet I did.

● ● ●

Alain 'Rollers' Rolland first walked into my office in late 1998. He told me he was doing a bit of reffing, and thought it might be an idea to take it seriously. At that point, he had been capped by Ireland in both XVs and Sevens. My initial thoughts were that he would be quite a catch, and if he was any good, the sky might be the limit.

Success has many fathers and failure none, and much later on, as many started to realise his very serious potential, just as many seemed to be the first to have seen him with the whistle in hand. The truth is different. Ned Cummins, a senior referee assessor in Leinster, had taken a stroll down to the lower pitches in Stradbrook, home to the Blackrock club. There, he came across Rollers helping out his club by refereeing a very junior match. Cummins liked what he saw, and told him to make sure to go and see me.

We knew each other well – I had reffed him many times

– he was a very chirpy scrum-half with plenty of opinions about his opponents' illegalities. On the touchline, his mother Helena was a very keen supporter. His number one fan in fact, and not beyond staring her own silent disapproval at me if I ever dared to penalise her son, who could, of course, do no wrong. It was all good-humoured fun.

At the time of our conversation, I was starting to fast-track talented referees, rather than making them do a long probation at the lower levels that had, until then, always been the norm. So we got Rollers started in early 1999, the year of the first professional World Cup. We filmed his performances, wired for sound, and although he wasn't great technically, it was clear that he had a wonderfully instinctive feel for the game. Next, he went into the All Ireland League; his first match was in the Suttonians club, again filmed. It was probably the club's biggest crowd to date, with plenty of assessors keen to get a good look at him, some approving of his rapid rise, others not.

Same thing for his first senior schools match in Donnybrook, where many referees wanted to see if he was really as good as we in the IRFU were claiming him to be. Father David Tyndall, a priest and very good referee to boot, had been doubtful, but he came up to me after the match and told me, 'Fair enough, he is excellent.'

This was not just fast-tracking, it was a bullet train, and Rollers successfully met every challenge we put before him. He showed no interest at all in the formal assessment system, he just wanted my opinion, and always went with it. Now, when most referees get coaching advice on anything from positioning to scrum management, it takes them at least several matches to stitch it all into their game plan. With Rollers, it was instant, he would immediately be refereeing to the new advice.

Within less than 18 months, he was the man in the middle for Wales 'A' v South Africa, and still people were frowning, this was too fast. For a moment, I thought maybe a slowdown might be best, but there was no logical reason to, and on we went.

From a standing start in 1999, he had been selected, alongside Dave McHugh, by the IRB for the 2003 World Cup in Australia. It had been just a four-year journey to the top group of the world's elite referees, and it got better. Following excellent performances in the pool stages, he was appointed to a quarter-final, England v Wales.

And by the time another four-year World Cup cycle had passed, that achievement would be bettered again as the great and good of rugby convened for France 2007.

Argentina once more became Ireland's nemesis, beating us 30–15 in the pool stages. They also beat France in the opening match, reffed by Englishman Tony Spreadbury, therefore topping the pool. We also lost to France and thus Eddie O'Sullivan's team crashed out before the knockout phase. Hopes had been high, and it was very dispiriting, despite the fact that it was an extremely tricky pool – don't forget that both France and Argentina reached the semifinal stage.

Often forgotten from that time was that Ireland played the French club Bayonne in a warm-up match. Considering France were in the same pool, with a game against them around the corner, it was completely ill-judged, even though Bayonne was convenient to Ireland's base in Bordeaux. That said, Ireland would have been happy enough with the appointment of a World Cup panel referee, Wayne Barnes.

It turned out to be a shocking battle, extremely hard to control, with the French club seemingly intent on softening up Ireland before the main event. Brian O'Driscoll was clearly targeted and very nearly put out of the tournament when punched in an off-the-ball incident. Others were left nursing serious bruises.

The accommodation arrangements for the Irish team were also far from ideal. While Bordeaux has a magical feel to it, they were staying in a hotel on the outskirts of the city – it was well-equipped, including a gym, but the taxi ride to get in and out of town for any sort of break couldn't have done much for morale.

The most seismic shock of 2007 was the elimination of New Zealand by France at the quarter-final stage, 18–20 in Cardiff. Wayne Barnes, still only 27 years old, had been entrusted with the match, but did not referee it well, with a very clear forward pass missed in the build-up to a crucial try by France. There were other controversial issues too, including a call to sin bin Kiwi centre Luke McAlister, France scoring a try and a penalty in his absence. It was an unnecessary appointment, one Barnes didn't really need at that stage of his career. Perhaps the thinking behind it was that New Zealand would win it easily, but that would have been to overlook the French propensity for turning the tables, particularly on the All Blacks.

The Kiwi press was vicious, vitriolic, as they tore into Wayne's performance; all of New Zealand was livid. I sat and listened to a small group of their supporters in a bistro in Paris and the anger and disbelief were intense. There was hatred in the air, Barnes was the target. Hard-earned cash had been spent on the trip and their plane had landed in Paris as the departing All Blacks flight was taking off, and many others were in the same boat, so to speak.

It all went way beyond the norms of rugby controversy, and the abuse Barnes received reached 'death threat' level. New Zealand premier Helen Clark even felt it necessary to publicly denounce the perpetrators.

As Paddy O'Brien had done eight years earlier, Barnes did exceptionally and admirably well to recover, build himself back and become one of the world's best and most respected referees. But New Zealand never forgot, much less forgave!

The Irish match officials selected for 2007 were referees Alain Rolland and Alan Lewis, together with assistant referee Simon McDowell.

Lewis and Rolland were two of the best in the world at that point and we travelled with a very definite referee objective for this World Cup. While you could not imagine two more different personalities, each was at the top of their game. I felt that either, or both, could reach at least the semi-final stages, with Rolland just the more accurate in terms of decision-making; but at that level it is very small margins indeed. So if Ireland weren't to progress, then we'd make every effort to have at least one Irishman there on final day.

And this despite being up against a hugely talented group of referees, which included Nigel Owens, Joël Jutge, Paul Honiss, Steve Walsh, Chris White, Jonathan Kaplan and Tony Spreadbury. All of those, plus the two Irishmen, could have reffed, at the very least, as far as the quarter-final stage. Paddy O'Brien, then IRB referee manger, and his selectors were spoilt for choice; that's a lot of referees capable of 'bringing the tournament home' and that sort of comfort may not exist when the next World Cup comes around.

Unlike the Ireland team, the Irish referees really cracked it; both were excellent in their early matches, and appointments to the knockouts followed. Rolland reffed the Australia v England quarter-final, a match won by English forward power and four Jonny Wilkinson penalties, with Australia getting the game's only try through Lote Tuqiri. Lewis was appointed to South Africa v Fiji's quarter-final.

Fiji had beaten Wales to get this far, and put in a very exciting performance but it was the Springbok pack that prevailed, in a 37–20 victory, although not before Fiji had staged a remarkable second-half comeback. Two tries in about a minute drew the sides level at 20–20, despite Fiji having a man in the sin bin. Desperate tackling just about kept the Fijians from getting any more, and it was a very relieved South African team that trundled off when Lewis called time. He had refereed extremely well, one of his best performances.

The semi-final appointments went to New Zealand's Steve Walsh and South Africa's Jonathan Kaplan, with Lewis and England's Chris White missing out.

And then, as we all remember, Rolland was appointed to the final, England v South Africa. This was as good as it can get, and it was something we had all striven to achieve, and believed could be done.

Like a lot of finals, this was a wary, pretty dour affair. Not a try was scored, though England came damn close, but South Africa won 15–6 to join Australia as twice-winners of the William Webb Ellis Cup. It needed very accurate refereeing, which Alain gave it; these matches are much more difficult to handle than open, free-flowing affairs.

The match itself was most notable for a very, very hard and long look at a potential England try by Mark Cueto. The TMO, Australian Stuart Dickinson, eventually ruled it out for the tightest of tight calls, the very edge of Cueto's boot considered to have shaved the touchline as the winger dived to score a try that may well have been awarded in a previous era.

After the tournament was over, we held a debrief, and concluded that, while Lewis would well have merited a semi-final, it was unrealistic to expect us to get four out of the seven knockout matches, so politically it wasn't really ever a runner.

Rollers performed in so many elite matches that it would be impossible to list them all. He was still going strong at the next World Cup in 2011 and was appointed to the France v Wales semi-final, to fill his full house of knockout matches.

Along the way, there were three Heineken Cup finals, including Wasps' win over Toulouse in Toulouse, when Rob Howley famously stole a try from under the nose of Clément Poitrenaud. Wary of conceding a five-metre scrum in the dying moments, Poitrenaud had dillied and dallied behind his own line, waiting a millisecond too long to ground the ball, and Howley pounced for the tournament-winning score.

Not at all a social animal, preferring to head off to the gym at any and every opportunity, Rollers was an extremely fit individual, never touching a drop of alcohol. Disciplined in everything he did, he once travelled to New Zealand on a Thursday for a Saturday Test match, returning immediately after the match to be in the office on Monday morning.

During that 2007 World Cup, he got special permission to return home for a couple of days to help his wife Lizzie clear out the kitchen before a new one could be installed. It's probably a very safe bet that he was the only one in the group who would have made such a choice.

Finishing his career with a total of 68 tier-one Tests, that

The Ref's Call

World Cup final and those three European finals, Alain Rolland has clearly been our most successful. But was he the best?

Without trying to dodge the question, my own view is that it's difficult to put much more than a sheet of paper between Lewis, McHugh and Rolland. On their day, the three of them were right up there with the best in the world, and various clubs, unions and, indeed, rugby fans would all have had their own favourites from that small group.

Chapter Eighteen

1 May 2008

International Rugby Board announces
12-month trial of experimental law variations

Whatever happens, whatever law changes are considered, nothing should be introduced to rugby union that could damage its greatest asset, its greatest attraction – that it is a game for players of all shapes and sizes.

When a union team arrive at the ground and get off their bus, most people can tell which players will tog out in the various positions. That's unlikely to be the case in rugby league, where most of the players are of an identical size.

The Ref's Call

I nodded in agreement listening, once again, to perceptive words of New Zealand native Lee Smith, who, in 1996, had taken up the role of director of development at the Dublin-based International Rugby Board, and also coached University College Dublin during his time in Ireland. Like anybody else who met Smith, I was fascinated by his deep insights into the game, but little was more persuasive than his bus analogy, it has stuck with me ever since.

And yet, when the experimental law variations were being proposed and championed, particularly from Australia, that very fundamental maxim seemed largely forgotten.

• • •

Every solution has a problem. Otherwise known as the law of unintended consequences, that type of consequence has reared its ugly head more than once in the annals of the laws of rugby union.

In general terms, there is a methodology for unions to offer suggestions about law changes, changes it sees as being for the betterment of the game, not just issues that it feels would suit its style of play better, although those have not been unknown to make their way onto the table for debate. These are then discussed among all the unions, and each union has to vote on the various proposals. Unlike the Brexit vote, more than a simple majority is required for a law change proposal to go to trial. Over the years, these proposals have generally never been too radical and, on that basis, the game has evolved, rather than being changed dramatically. World Rugby (which the International Rugby Board changed its name to in 2014) are responsible for collating and coding all such proposals and for collecting the results of the vote.

Law change proposals are then trialled as experiments in various tournaments across both hemispheres so that their effect on the game can be measured, before anything is cemented into law. In theory, this seems like a good idea, but, like all trials or experiments, until they reach the top end of the game, it is extremely difficult to know what the outcome and the effect on the game will be.

At the beginning of any law trial, players and coaches are mostly very compliant as they try to get their heads around new styles of play, and to understand that some things, previously allowed, are now illegal; and vice-versa. By the time these changes get to the top end of the game, coaches and players are working out how best they can be used to gain an advantage over their opponents, and that is fair enough. But that is where the problems to the solutions start to show up, and what happens next is often not what has happened in the law trials. Unintended consequences.

Rugby union differs from the NFL in the United States and from rugby league in many ways, but particularly around the tackle. The latter two get rid of any problems in this area by calling a halt to proceedings when a tackle is made; in the sharpest of contrasts, rugby union plays on at the tackle, and the contest for possession at the breakdown is a fundamental characteristic of the game. The downside is that the breakdown has always been difficult to referee, and accounts (together with the scrum and foul play, albeit for different reasons) for the vast majority of penalty kicks. So the thing that differentiates the sport from other field games is the tackle and breakdown area, while, at the same time, it also has become a very contentious part of the game.

In the mid -2000s, people were looking hard at the game, and many felt that the existing methodology for proposing law changes was too laborious, and that perhaps more radical change was needed; faster ball from the breakdown was essential to get better, faster continuity of play. At least, that was the thinking.

So the International Rugby Board set up a Laws Project Group (LPG), under the chairmanship of Scotland's Bill Nolan, an IRB member. It was a strong, knowledgeable group and included former international coaches, chief among them Rod McQueen, who had led the Wallabies to World Cup glory in 1999. There was also Nolan's fellow Scot Richie Dixon, France's Pierre Villepreux and South Africa's Ian McIntosh. Others on the LPG were former All-Black captain Graham Mourie, and Bruce Cook and Paddy O'Brien from the IRB, with the whole exercise to be facilitated by the governing body's Steve Griffiths. For some reason, which I have never quite fathomed, there was no representative from either England or Ireland; but their involvement would come later, though by then it was nearly to be too late.

The LPG came up with a series of proposals, known as the experimental law variations; in short, the ELVs. The most controversial among them were:

- Most penalty kicks, even those around the breakdown, would be replaced by free kicks.

- The maul could be collapsed, something that hitherto had been considered dangerous.

- A team could put any number it wished into a lineout, taking away the rationale that the team throwing in decided the maximum number.

The ELV's were trialled in several competitions, notably the Australian Rugby Championship and Super Rugby, during 2008. In the northern hemisphere, law trials are more complex to introduce, as players move in and out of different competitions. The results of these trials were very carefully noted by the IRB, as were the opinions garnered from coaches and players; I remember reading page after page of these comments, they were all filled with 'green', indicating approval. It seemed that all of these ELVs were working, and were going to be for the good.

Yet, I was following Super Rugby closely and found

myself becoming ever more sceptical as to what exactly some of the major proposals were actually doing to the game. First of all, it seemed that the maul was fast disappearing, whereas the LPG made the counterargument that there were the same number. *Go figure*, I thought. So I did go figure – referee development manager Dave McHugh and I spent many evenings and weekends doing exactly that; it resulted in an anecdotal report and short video to the Six Nations committee.

They were very much persuaded by the presentation, but an anecdotal, opinion-based report would have no chance of overturning the vast amount of contradictory, notated evidence of those in favour. And that is where England came in; they said that they would finance new research and produce a report that would show if their conclusions supported the data from down south or not. In the event, it did not.

Kevin Bowring had been coach of Wales and was now working with the RFU in charge of England's high-performance coach development; there was little he didn't know about the game and he led the research. We met on several occasions to discuss the issues, but he was very much running the show and did a terrific job.

In March 2009, a meeting took place to ratify the ELVs, but before any vote could be taken, The IRB invited Bowring to present the case for the opposition. Some from the southern hemisphere were less than impressed, and said it was too late to introduce new so-called findings. But that was quickly overruled; all evidence, no matter how new, needed to be heard and considered.

Bowring gave an unemotional, intelligent and practical presentation of great depth; and shortly after he started speaking, the then-CEO of Australia Rugby, John O'Neill, left the meeting. Perhaps, even so early, he could see the writing on the wall.

Yes, Bowring said, the number of mauls hadn't changed much, but where they took place definitely had. They were now mostly in defensive positions on the pitch and led to more defensive kicking, which, in turn, led to more kicks. The attacking maul had disappeared, and one of rugby's only three ways of moving the ball forward was disappearing with it. Defences were strung out across the field more than ever before, as the need to commit players to defend an attacking maul was gone. The back line was facing more defenders and, finding it difficult to move forward, were more likely to kick, so dynamic attacking play was discouraged by de-powering the maul.

Similar to the scrum, where eight defenders are tied in, the maul should provide great attacking opportunities, when defenders are forced to join in significant numbers to defend it.

The number of kicks at goal, and hence points scored from penalties, had reduced, but the number of free kicks had soared, often as many as 30 to 40 per game; offences and stoppages at the breakdown were, as a consequence, increasing hugely. This confirmed the anecdotal research we'd done in Dublin, that fast ball was only coming from quick-tap free kicks and not, anymore, from the breakdown itself. The shape of the game, and the way it was played, would have taken a dramatic turn for the worse had these changes gone through.

Looking around the room, I could see people who, previously in the 'for' camp but who had been persuaded by the factual and detailed arguments put forward by Bowring, were starting to realise that some of the ELVs were not all they were made out to be.

After the conference, the IRB announced that the majority of the ELVs had been voted in, and indeed some of the smaller, but very useful, changes were approved universally. Keeping the three-quarters back five metres from scrums, and allowing quick throw-ins from touch to be thrown backwards, have both worked well. As has the direct kick to touch from a ball brought back into the 22 being 'penalised' by the lineout taking place opposite where the ball was kicked. But the big game-changing proposals did not see the light of day, nor should they have.

After several years of dedicated work, and having being convinced that they were on the right track, the Laws Project Group was disbanded. As to the merits of their radical proposals, perhaps some of them still think that they were right, but none of these have ever been re-proposed by any union, north or south of the equator, and that tells its own story.

Chapter Nineteen

13 November 2009

Wales v Samoa in Cardiff
(Autumn international)

*The feelings I had on my own first international are the same
for everyone who referees their first Test in Cardiff.*

*The enormity of the moment, the atmosphere, the singing, it
all stays with you forever. There can be no doubt but that it is
the most atmospheric, emotional stadium in world rugby.*

*Fitzgibbon's debut there in 2009 was no different, but
having had a hand in his development, it was a nostalgic
moment for me.*

• • •

The Ref's Call

With McHugh, Lewis and Rolland now firmly established, we were keen to keep the conveyor belt rolling and, in 2003, we noticed that there were two young men in Limerick who were refereeing far better than their level of experience: Peter Fitzgibbon and George Clancy. We brought them quickly onto the IRFU panels.

Fitzgibbon, like Keith Earls, came from the Thomond club, and he had an excellent and instinctive feel for the role. On the pitch, his communication was aided by absolutely fluent French, and this would help him hugely when, in November 2011, he refereed the local derby between Bayonne and Biarritz in France's Top 14. These two mighty Basque rugby clubs are within 10 kilometres of each other, and the rivalry is always highly intense.

French international Imanol Harinordoquy (a winner of three Grand Slams) togged out at number eight for Biarritz, with his father Lucien sitting in the stand. Or at least that's where he started the match. Following an early brawl, Imanol and Bayonne back-row Jean-Jo Marmouyet were having a fair old go at each other, and this was not to the liking of Harinordoquy Père. Moving quickly from his seat, he joined in the fray, deciding that his six-foot-four son, weighing 105 kilos, needed his paternal assistance. Hardly likely, but he couldn't restrain himself.

His involvement, unsurprisingly, was short lived, cut down by a classic tackle from Bayonne number 10, Benjamin Boyet. Thankfully, he was unhurt and was led off the pitch, certain to face a lot of music. Fitzgibbon then set about calming things down, speaking to both teams in their native tongue, which certainly helped. For the record, Biarritz squeezed home 21–19.

Then came a Test debut in Cardiff, with Wales – despite wearing a distinctly odd yellow kit – eking out a 17–13 win against Samoa. An exemplary yellow card to Samoan full-back Lolo Lui after 90 seconds set the tone and gave notice that tackling needed to be according to the book. I was delighted to watch him come through with flying colours.

He had already performed really well in Wales at the Junior World Cup (JWC) the previous autumn and his arrival at tier-one Test level was absolutely merited. The JWC had been won by New Zealand, beating England in the final, which was refereed by Fitzgibbon.

At this point the IRFU referee department was producing elite referees at a healthy rate of knots, and the competition for matches could not have been greater. Otherwise, Fitzgibbon's talent would surely have seen him appointed to many more Test matches than he would actually achieve.

John 'The Bull' Hayes is undoubtedly the most famous rugby man to come out of Bruff RFC, where he played before moving to the Shannon club, collecting an astonishing 105 Irish caps, two Lions tours and over 200 appearances for Munster. For a prop forward, whose first love was hurling, his career was truly magnificent.

Out of Bruff too came another hurler, referee George Clancy. The name also resonates with followers of Irish history – for it was Clancy's great-grand-uncle, the Limerick mayor of the same name, who along with the previous incumbent Michael O'Callaghan and a young volunteer, Joseph O'Donohue, were targeted by the Black and Tans in a well-known incident during the War of Independence. The three men were murdered in Limerick on the night of 7 March 1921.

The first thing we noticed about Clancy was his exceptional pace, although, in the beginning, he would often run himself out of good positions. But he was a very quick learner, and with intense coaching, alongside watching very successful role models in people like McHugh, Lewis, Courtney and Rolland, he made rapid progress, and leap-frogged through the ranks.

In 2010, Clancy was in Cardiff, where he was in charge for one of the most epic finishes ever seen in a Six Nations match. Wales trailed 14–24 to Scotland as the last five minutes approached. It seemed all over, but Scotland's infringing earned a couple of yellow cards, and nor had they reckoned with the pace and guile of Leigh Halfpenny and Shane Williams. A converted try from each in the last three minutes saw that very comfortable lead overturned, and a bemused Scotland headed to the dressing rooms, losers by 24–31.

Like all referees, there was no avoiding a few bumps and bruises along the way for Clancy. In February 2009, the year of Ireland's second Grand Slam, he went to Paris for his Six Nations debut. France's opponents Scotland were very unhappy with the decision to award a try to Fulgence

Ouedraogo, the crucial pass from Maxime Médard looking distinctly doubtful, but Clancy had been knocked over in the buildup. Rightly, he consulted with his assistant Wayne Barnes before giving the try, but the moment still created its share of controversy.

A South Africa v New Zealand match in 2011 saw him receive a stern rebuke from the IRB for going outside the TMO protocol to rule out a Jimmy Cowan try for a weakened New Zealand team, as they went down 18–5. But All Blacks coach Graham Henry said he did not have a problem with the decision; the pass from Israel Dagg to Cowan was pretty clearly forward. In those days, the TMO was not supposed to be consulted on issues such as forward passing; nonetheless, it looked very much like the right call had been made. And thankfully, the pragmatic Henry would not allow himself to be annoyed at that outcome.

Clancy and Henry would cross paths again later that year, when New Zealand hosted the seventh Rugby World Cup. The country was getting everything ready for the tournament when the tragic Christchurch earthquake struck. That meant the city, sadly but inevitably, lost its scheduled pool matches and quarter-finals.

The Limerick man was selected, along with Alain Rolland, giving Ireland two referees, with Simon McDowell again travelling as an assistant official. Clancy received the signal honour of being appointed to the opening match of the competition, New Zealand v Tonga.

Ireland, under coach Declan Kidney, got into their stride

quickly. In what looked like the dawning of a great hope, Ireland topped their pool, including an excellent win over Australia, and thus avoided a quarter-final against South Africa, meeting Wales instead.

This team was still very much the golden generation and, with a new coach in Kidney, confidence levels were very high – maybe too high. Ireland have probably never fielded a better team, but it failed to do the business on that night in Wellington's 'Cake Tin' stadium. Wales had much the better of things, and there can have been no complaints whatsoever with referee Craig Joubert's handling of it. The result was Ireland 10, Wales 22, with Wales winning the try count three to one. A dream was well and truly shattered; it had been, after all the hope, a false dawn.

But the tournament was not short of referee controversies. Decisions, or non-decisions, may or may not have had a bearing on the outcome of several key matches. It's pretty much a truism to say that, either in soccer or rugby World Cups, there will inevitably be at least one debatable or poor referee performance.

The most infamous of all was in the soccer World Cup in 1978, delivered by Welshman Clive Thomas. With their game against Sweden poised at 1–1 entering stoppage time, Brazil were awarded a corner. It was perfectly struck by Nelinho, Zico rose to meet it, and headed the ball home for the winning score. Alas, a goal it was not. Thomas, deciding that full-time had arrived a split second before Zico struck the ball goalwards, had blown the final whistle and set off for the tunnel. On 90 minutes and six seconds, it was a calculation of impossible preciseness, and Thomas would not referee a World Cup match again.

Nothing that Bryce Lawrence did in the 2011 quarter-final, South Africa v Australia, came within a country mile of Thomas' dreadful decision, but holders South Africa were dumped out of the tournament by a score of 11–9, and had a lot to say about the referee's performance in the aftermath. Aussie wing-forward David Pocock played a stormer, but some of the breakdown refereeing did leave question marks. Lawrence, to his credit, was honest and open about it later, admitting that he missed things that he should have picked up. There were only about 10 penalties in the match, and a few more would have helped him, and arguably the Springboks, greatly.

Lawrence retired the following year, having felt it impossible to referee in South Africa in the SANZAR Super Rugby competition. Such was the level of anger among Springbok supporters, there was a risk to his safety, and he was right not to travel there. Lawrence would go on to become the New Zealand national referee manager, a position previously held by his father Keith, who also was an international referee. That is quite some father–son achievement.

Another New Zealander, Steve Walsh, refereed the shock of the tournament. Having accounted for Italy in 1999, Tonga went a step further when they defeated France 19–14, in what is one of the most extraordinary and un-expected results in the history of the World Cup. France, nonetheless, escaped from the pool stages and went on to the final, but they surely thanked their lucky stars that the Tongans had suffered an upset of their own in losing to Canada, otherwise the story of this World Cup would have been very different.

That Tonga win showed, again, that referees in any sport must never presume anything. Just referee whatever comes up, however unexpected, and Walsh did just that on a historic day. As Dave McHugh had in 1999.

In the Wales v France semi-final, there was the well-documented story of Sam Warburton's early red card, correctly delivered by Alain Rolland, though very many in Wales will never agree. Despite it, Wales only lost very narrowly, 9–8. In fact, they had a very late chance to win, a long-range Leigh Halfpenny penalty grazing the underside of the crossbar. It looked an incorrect call by the referee against prop Nicolas Mas for offside at a ruck and, if kicked, the French would have been the team with the very serious grievance.

The English team provided unnecessary controversy off the pitch with their drinking, led by captain Mike Tindall, at a bar which was holding some kind of rowdy competition. It said nothing for their professionalism. England subsequently exited tamely to France in the quarter-final; going 16–0 down early on proved too much, with the match finishing at 19–12. While their head coach Martin Johnson would no doubt have been bitterly disappointed at the defeat, the off-field carry on must have, inwardly, made him livid. He resigned his position following the tournament, just before his position was to be reviewed by the RFU. In truth, the wonderful World Cup-winning captain had not delivered in a very different role.

South African Craig Joubert had caught the eye during the tournament, extremely fit and decisive. It had been no surprise to see him selected, nor to see him rewarded with both a quarter-final and a semi-final. But when it was announced that he was appointed to the France v New Zealand final, more than a few eyebrows were raised; this is a match for the last quartile of a referee's career, when everything to be experienced is already in the locker. Not, though, for so early on, and at 34 years of age he was, and remains, the youngest referee to be appointed to the final.

In the event, Joubert seemed very tense, and France will have rued some tackle and scrum decisions that went against them, not to mention a number of decisions that they felt they should have got but didn't. The refereeing was later openly criticised by several French players, and Joubert shipped plenty of it in the media. The referee selectors, though, must take some of the blame for putting him in at the deepest of deep ends.

It all wasn't helped by New Zealand producing their worst rugby of the competition to scrape home by 8–7, having already beaten France at a canter in the pool stages, 37–17. It was scant consolation for France that they produced their best performance of the tournament yet fell short at the final hurdle once more.

Chapter Twenty

6 February 2009

Ireland v France in Ashbourne
(First day of that year's Women's Six Nations)

The Ireland team's dressing room must have been very quiet, the talk and the preparations were over. Nothing left to say, just things to do.

They were ready, and there was a collective resolve to do something very special, get a result never before achieved. As the past had proved, beating France was no easy task.

The Irish captain led them out of the pavilion and onto the pitch. Eighty minutes later when they returned, the deed had been done. Happiness and relief were unconfined.

Joy Neville was that captain, and the French colours had been lowered by the squeakiest of narrow margins, 7–5.

Trailing perilously by 0–5 with just over five minutes left, Fiona Coghlan got over for the vital try, with the equally vital conversion slotted by Niamh Briggs.

History had been made.

• • •

As the men's game turned professional in the 1995 season, Irish women were also taking their first steps into international competition, with the inaugural Home Nations tournament launching in February the following year. Becoming the Five Nations with the addition of France for the 1999 edition, Ireland were actually replaced by Spain in 2000 and 2001 before returning, alongside newcomers Italy, to complete the present-day Six Nations line-up in 2002.

It hadn't been an easy beginning for Ireland, with five wooden spoons in their first seven competitions. But things began looking up in the tournament's second decade as a new generation of players began to emerge. A first win arrived in 2005, 11–6 against Wales, before Scotland were finally beaten, 18–6 in 2007.

It was two years before heads really started to turn as France arrived to Ashbourne and Ireland were led to a famous victory by Joy Neville.

The Neville family are steeped in rugby: Joy's father Ger played for Bohemians, and in 2007 her brother Paul captained Garryowen to an extraordinary treble of both the All Ireland League and Cup, plus the Munster Cup for good measure. He also played for the Ireland Sevens, as did his sister.

Neville had a simply stellar playing career for Ireland, which started in 2003, and finished in 2013 when Ireland completed their graduation to top-level rugby by cleanly sweeping up all of the available titles: the Triple Crown, the Six Nations and the Grand Slam. The team would go on to do what the men have yet to achieve by reaching the World Cup semi-finals the following year, with a famous 17–14 win over New Zealand the highlight en route to a fourth-place finish.

While Neville had retired after the 2013 Six Nations win, her appearances at the previous two World Cups, plus a huge total of 70 caps, meant there was pretty much nothing left to achieve in the game. Ah, but wait.

While Neville was busy playing for Ireland, other women had already taken up the whistle, with Dubliner Helen O'Reilly, under the initial tutelage of Dave O'Brien, breaking through some glass ceilings of her own. She became the first woman to referee in the All Ireland League when she took charge of Sunday's Well v Kanturk in 2015, and was also the first woman to officiate as an assistant in the Pro14, Munster v Zebre.

The French National Centre of Rugby situated at Marcoussis, to the south of Paris near Orly airport, is a state-of-the-art facility. Rooms and dining are of five-star quality, but when the gates close behind you, you are 'in' – rather like being at a boarding school in the middle of nowhere. The French teams prepare and train there, but because there is nowhere to go, and the centre of Paris is just out of reach at some 25 kilometres away – it is more often referred to as Marcatraz by the players.

The 2014 Women's World Cup was played in its entirety, in Marcoussis. Helen refereed a semi-final there and was narrowly pipped for the final by the excellent Australian Amy Perret. Nobody had a clue, then, that Ireland would very soon after referee the final of that tournament.

In 2013, Neville had decided to hang up her boots to spend more time with her partner, now wife, Simona Coppola. While not exactly reaching for her slippers, she was determined to take a long break from the game; nobody was more deserving.

But one person had another idea altogether: Dave McHugh. Macker knew several things – that Neville had retired, that she had fantastic instinctive knowledge of rugby and that she could be as least as good a referee as she was a player; in other words, a damn good one, out of the top drawer. It was a great bit of crystal-balling.

Ostensibly, McHugh reported to me in the IRFU, but we worked very much as a team, with different but complementary roles. We'd often joke that he'd mine the diamonds, and I would cut and polish them.

The phone rang. 'What d'ya think of Joy Neville? I'm thinking of getting her to try reffing.'

The Ref's Call

My reply was quick. 'That'd be some trick, do your very best.'

So off he went, and the next phone he rang was Joy Neville's. They had several long conversations, but there was no immediate rush to take the bait. The best he got was, 'Give me a call in six months,' probably to get him off the line. But Dave did exactly that and, to the day, if not to the minute, Joy's phone rang again.

As is her wont, she had been thinking about the idea. And this time the answer was, 'Yes, but if I don't like it, I'm not staying.' That went without saying, and the deal was done. We knew that this was a real gem; and this time I proposed that Dave would be the main cutter and polisher. After all, he'd got her in, so let's see what he could do. Well, as history tells us, they did a fantastic job together. Many a duck has been slower to take to water than the time it took Joy to take to refereeing.

One of the assurances she wanted was that, if she turned out to be good, neither provincial politics nor anything else would get in her way. The message was the same as I had given to Alain Rolland: 'We'll go as fast as you can.' Later on, we heard that she had asked the opinion of a so-called senior rugby man if she could ever referee in the AIL Division 1. The unedifying reply, 'Not in my lifetime, I'm afraid', far from putting Neville off the idea, just made her more determined.

The first thing to say is that both Joy and Helen brought so much to the table as referees, both on and off the pitch.

In meetings of the IRFU panels, they showed knowledge and understanding. Everyone was very accepting of these two new refs on the block; if some weren't, it was never evident. The key thing was that they were not just token women in what, until then, had been the preserve of men. Everybody appreciated that they were just very fine referees and there on merit.

The IRFU panels are about 50 referees strong and these two were an integral part of that number, never for a moment out of place. One of my mantras has always been that we must strive to be the best, but that we must enjoy ourselves and have fun along the way; otherwise what's the point? Neville and O'Reilly bought into that in a big way.

Neville was particularly 'high level', very willing to be first with the suggested answer in role-playing situations. Mostly, she was correct but, when she wasn't, she would jot down the correct rationale and approach, learning, learning non-stop.

When Neville moved into the high-performance unit, a very select number of about seven or eight, she remained the same, always a knowledgeable contributor, and became as much a part of the furniture as any of the other top refs.

So, having signed up, and armed with a few watches and whistles, Joy Neville set out on a new pathway that was actually to become her second road to fame and to renewed recognition across the rugby world.

I've often thought that scrum-halves and back-row forwards have to know the game inside out. They know and have performed every trick in the book, including some of the unseen, dark arts, and Neville's number eight experience stood her in very good stead. Not everybody can successfully translate this knowledge to refereeing, but if they can, then it is a case of the finest poachers becoming the finest of gamekeepers.

Add in a dollop of very serious pace and athleticism, and you have a recipe that only the chef can muck up. And McHugh, whose inability in the kitchen is the stuff of legend, did not muck it up.

Progress was lightning fast, and breakthrough followed breakthrough.

The journey began in December 2013 with a friendly under-15s match, St Munchin's v CBC. Boys who played in that match would never have guessed what great heights the referee that day would reach. Following that were Munster Senior Schools Cup matches, and then next up on her checklist was the All Ireland League, when, on 12 November 2016, Joy completely defied that 'not in my lifetime' prediction by refereeing her first Division 1 match, between Cork Constitution and Clontarf.

Honours in the men's game started to pile up. She even had the resolve, and the ability, to travel to Wales and referee Ebbw Vale v Pontypridd. These 'old-fashioned' fixtures can be a graveyard but not for Neville. To be accepted as a referee by these tough-as-teak men from the valleys is not easy; to be accepted as a woman referee is quite something.

In fact, as time went on people were no longer surprised

to see her tog out and take her place in the middle for men's rugby. Neville then became the first woman to referee a men's professional match in a European competition, Bordeaux-Bègles against Russian side Enisei-STM in the Challenge Cup. As milestones hurtled by, she became a regular in the Guinness Pro14, and was one of a handful of IRFU referees to be offered a professional contract in 2017.

Ireland had been awarded the 2017 Women's World Cup, and ran a very good tournament across the whole island. The IRFU hoped that this would demonstrate their organisational abilities as they would bid later, albeit unsuccessfully, for the 2023 RWC.

Having played the sold-out pool matches in Dublin, the semi-final and final moved up north. New Zealand and England qualified for the final, with the former winning 41–32. I doubt very much if the referee selectors took more than a few moments to decide that the best referee for that showpiece would be Neville.

It was a moment of great pride not just for referees, but for everybody connected with the game when Joy ran out into a jam-packed Kingspan Stadium. There were 17,115 spectators in the ground, and another 2.5 million watching on TV. What an atmosphere those two great teams generated and what a match.

In the midst of all of that, World Rugby came calling, with news that Joy Neville was a contender to receive the prestigious Referee of the Year award 2017. So her next trip took her to the ceremony in Monte Carlo, and she came home with that glittering prize. And all that just four years after Macker had made his second phone call.

When Covid-19 locked down most things, elite sport continued, and Neville became a much-sought-after television match official in men's Test rugby, including at the Six Nations. TMO-ing, as we all too regularly see, is a very difficult role; but she took to it very much in her usual stride.

In autumn 2020, Neville became the first woman to be on the team of officials for a major Test match, bringing the same intuitive knowledge and decisiveness that she takes to the field to that role too.

After English second-row Maro Itoje plunged over the French line in the 2021 Six Nations, referee Andrew Brace ruled 'no try', a decision that, if upheld, would have had a hugely negative impact on his career. It had been a tricky enough day for him when he reffed the same teams in the previous autumn's Nations Cup, but things had gone very well for him this time. However, a match-altering decision would have sent all that good work down the drain.

However, Neville had noticed something, and quickly reviewed things. Yes, by the time Brace had seen the action, the ball was indeed held up, but had it been briefly touched down just before French hands got beneath it? Indeed it had, and advice came from the TMO that the on-field decision needed to be changed. That was teamwork at its very best.

And all of this was performed in the highly charged, pressurised atmosphere of a vital match, for the vital score.

When you referee a match, there is an instinctive flow to your thoughts and decisions, to your concentration. The TMO, on the other hand, follows the game at arm's length, watching the action on several screens, one in real time, one running some several seconds later. Powers of concentration need to be very carefully honed and maintained over the whole match. A referee can take a breather if there's a break in play, say for an injury, but at this point the TMO will be poring over replays to see if there's anything amiss that caused that injury. Joy Neville might well have a master's in multitasking.

Chapter Twenty-One

7 November 2017

The High Court, Phoenix Street, Dublin
(Dave McHugh v IRFU)

As my friend and colleague's business in the High Court reached its conclusion and vindicated him, my own feelings were of sadness and also of anger.

It was an extraordinary saga, and the most difficult of times for Macker who, alone, found himself in a pitched battle against a major sporting organisation. The whole thing was not handled well by a body that has always prided itself as an employer par excellence.

If this termination had been carried out properly, then I imagine it would also have saved the IRFU a lot of money, but no one saw fit to manage things otherwise.

Owen Doyle

*Had someone even considered taking him out for a coffee to
explain that a different direction was preferred and that,
sadly, they had to let him go but would come up with a decent
package, I'm certain the High Court could have been avoided.*

• • •

When Johnny Lacey decided to give the whistle a go, he
already had a very impressive rugby pedigree in the bag,
having collected a host of playing honours.

A regular try-scorer and five-time All Ireland League
winner with Shannon, he would later join Alain Rolland
as one of two Irish referees who both played and refereed
in the Heineken Cup, having notched up five tries for
Munster in that competition. Selected for Ireland at both
'A' and Sevens level, he fell short of a full cap, an omission
that would be rectified later as a referee.

Lacey progressed from a standing refereeing start in 2007
to the European Challenge Cup just three seasons later.
Three more years passed quickly as he climbed the ladder
steadily and, in 2012, England v Barbarians came his way,
with his Six Nations start in 2014 for Wales v Italy.

While he had refereed many big matches up to that
point, he appreciated the advice that this would be a
very different experience from anything he had so far
encountered. Together, we prepared very thoroughly, and

his performance reflected the pre-match work. It was yet another example of always planning, preparing and leaving no stone unturned.

The previous year, there had been lots of talk about referees not facing any consequences for below-par performances, but it was a real shock when we learned that George Clancy had been left out of the 2013 Six Nations. Such a setback might have endangered his future but, having knuckled down, he was straight back the following season, alongside Lacey.

Both would deservedly make the referee squad for the 2015 World Cup, where George Clancy would chat about rugby with the Queen at a reception in Buckingham Palace. What better signal that people had been able to move on from that terrible night in 1921 when Crown forces took his great-grand-uncle's life.

It was Clancy's second World Cup, having already been honoured with the referee duties for the 2011 edition's opening match, New Zealand v Tonga. By the time his international career came to its conclusion, he had been involved in many Test matches, both north and south of the equator, and had overcome the challenges presented by Type 1 diabetes – a true example to anyone who may doubt what can be done. Not bad going at all for the hurler from Bruff.

The draw for the 2015 World Cup, for reasons I never understood, took place all of three years earlier – and much had changed in the rankings when the tournament came around. England found themselves in a 'group of death', which contained the teams ranked two, three and four in the world, namely Australia, themselves and Wales. It wasn't the only reason why they went out at the pool stages – the only host team ever to have done so – but it most certainly didn't help.

They played poorly, and it was to see the disbandment of their coaching staff, including names who would later become very well known to Irish rugby fans: Stuart Lancaster, Andy Farrell, Mike Catt and Graham Rowntree. With Fiji and Uruguay making up the numbers in the pool, England realistically had to defeat either one of Wales or Australia to advance but failed to do so, albeit the match against Wales was lost by just three points, 28–25. It was a stunning win for Warren Gatland's men, who were 10 points behind with half an hour left. The loss of Ben Youngs to injury didn't help the English cause and a chance to draw the match in the last few minutes was turned down by captain Chris Robshaw, who elected to go for touch rather than a kick at goal.

The loss of another player saw England's chances against Australia evaporate, but this time it was self-inflicted. Owen Farrell's petulant off-the-ball wiping out of Matt Giteau saw him banished for the last 10 minutes by dint of a yellow card. It may well have been red but Giteau, closing out the match with a last-minute try, twisted the knife. Their 33–13 loss meant the host's tournament was over before it had really begun.

The Ref's Call

Australia had been very fortunate to get a very late penalty award from Craig Joubert in the quarter-final against Scotland. Joubert signalled the sanction for an offside when Scotland's Jon Welsh played the ball following a knock-on – a decision that World Rugby later confirmed as an error. The ball had hit Australian player Nick Phipps after the initial knock-on, meaning a scrum rather than a penalty would have been the correct decision. It had been a scintillating match, and it was very sad that it ended in this way, the kick giving Australia their win by 35–34.

Joubert, undoubtedly feeling huge pressure, and perhaps realising something was seriously amiss, ran from the pitch as soon as he blew the final whistle; it was a shame. He retired after the 2016 Olympics, still a very young man, and went on to join World Rugby's referee development and performance review group.

Michael Cheika brought his Australian team as far as the final, when the All Blacks retained their crown, 34–17, with Nigel Owens receiving the ultimate, and deserved, honour of refereeing it.

The Ireland team, with Joe Schmidt in charge for his first World Cup, topped their pool having had a very good win over France, 24–9. Thus, they avoided New Zealand in the quarters and headed to Cardiff to take on Argentina.

Ireland, though, were suffering badly in the medical room and had already lost key players to injury, including captain Paul O'Connell and Johnny Sexton, plus back-rowers Sean O'Brien and Peter O'Mahony. No doubt they knew they were up against it, and that Argentina were no slouches, having given the All Blacks a good run for their money in the pool stages. But nobody could have foreseen the concession of two very early tries, which put the Pumas into a 17-point lead after just 13 minutes, with yet another Irish injury seeing Tommy Bowe leave the field. While his replacement, Luke Fitzgerald, did very well, it was yet another blow to morale to see Bowe leaving the pitch.

While there was great credit due to Ireland for fighting back to 20–23, they would not score again. Argentina had more from the bench and, with their back three in terrific form, they scored two tries and a total of 17 unanswered points in the last half an hour. The final tally of 43–20 did not flatter Argentina, but, oh, those injuries. Nobody could blame the referee, Frenchman Jérôme Garcès, but it was yet another quarter-final defeat. Déjà vu.

When Garcès looks back at his career, he will also remember being involved in probably the greatest upset of all the Rugby World cups. With Japan's match against South Africa entering the final minute, the Brave Blossoms needed a try for the most impossible of victories and, to the astonishment of all, they got it. They moved the ball fast from right to left, the final pass going to Karne Hesketh, who crashed over for the match-winner, as far out in the corner as it's possible to be without being in touch.

The Japanese coach, Eddie Jones, had entered Hesketh into the fray just a few moments earlier. Given this spectacular result, and England's dismal performance, Jones can't have been overly surprised to receive a phone call from the RFU. He became England head coach shortly after the tournament and immediately led England to their first Grand Slam in 13 years.

Meanwhile, Lacey had been appointed to the bronze final, between South Africa and Argentina. These matches are notoriously difficult to officiate, as most teams would just prefer to go home when they've lost a semi-final, but it's a nice earner for World Rugby, appealing also to over 50,000 supporters who bought tickets for the match in London's Olympic stadium. It wasn't easy refereeing, but it was an opportunity for Lacey to lay down a marker for the future. The match was notable as the last international played by Springboks Victor Matfield and Schalk Burger, who finished their careers with a 24–13 win.

Although South Africa won easily enough, they spent much of the time trying to manoeuvre a try for Bryan Habana, which would have edged him just one ahead of Jonah Lomu in the all-time World Cup try-scoring stakes. While the bronze medal was won, that mission failed.

It was hoped that this was a definite springboard for Lacey to reach the knockout stages the next time around, in Japan, but it was not to be.

My own time in the IRFU had been due to finish with my scheduled retirement in late 2013, but things were continuing apace in the referee department. As we were just halfway through a World Cup cycle at that stage, it was agreed that I'd stay on until the conclusion of the 2015 tournament, and continue to manage and coach the elite referees who were in contention for selection.

Part of my brief during this extension was to draw up a plan for when I did eventually step aside. My view was that more of the same was exceptionally important, and I proposed that Dave McHugh would take over. He and I had an amicable discussion with the recently appointed IRFU performance director David Nucifora and the proposal was approved. It was also agreed that I would stay on and assist McHugh with elite-referee coaching, which I did until my own role came to a natural conclusion in 2017.

On my last day, I walked down the steps of number 10–12, which is at the far end of Lansdowne Road from number 62, those old premises having become long since outgrown. The new offices are now pretty much packed out, and how different things are. The committee system had become no longer fit for purpose and don't hold anything like the sway they used to. The professional game is very largely in the hands of one man, the performance director. That was change indeed.

However, McHugh's long involvement with the union, first as a leading referee and then working for – or rather with – me, also ended in 2017 in extremely contentious circumstance.

As planned, he had succeeded me in 2015, but a total of over 20 years' service came to a shuddering halt two years later. Calling into Lansdowne Road for a planned meeting that October with his boss David Nucifora, he left the building very shortly afterwards, dismissed, totally unexpectedly. The brief explanation was that a recent independent review into the referee department had indicated a change of direction. Also present at that quick meeting were the heads of HR and legal, respectively Aileen Bailey and Declan McPhillips.

When interviewed by the independent review team, I had told them that he was the key cog in the whole process and needed to remain in charge. Instead, they decided to let a very good man go.

It is a matter of public record that McHugh sought and got an ex-parte injunction at the High Court stopping his dismissal, and that the whole matter was later settled out of court less than a week later. As this was a confidential settlement, I have no idea about the amount, but it was undoubtedly significantly more than if a 'softer' approach had been taken; add in legal costs and a pretty hefty – and avoidable – expense had to be met. A very positive alternative would have been to move him sideways into a coaching-only role.

Following his parting with the IRFU, others saw his value and sought him out, including World Rugby. The Welsh union asked him to become involved with Nigel Owens, who he assisted in getting to an unexpected semi-final spot in RWC 2019. He has also gone on to coach referees in Georgia, who have, incidentally, now more full-time referees than Ireland.

When Johnny Lacey's name did not appear on the list of referees for the 2019 Six Nations, it was clear that he had slipped quite a bit in World Rugby's pecking order, and the writing was beginning to appear on the wall. The bad news continued with his omission from the group chosen for the 2019 World Cup in Japan. Lacey called time on his illustrious career that same year, moving into the key role of high performance referee coach in the IRFU's referee department, headed up by Dudley Phillips who had been appointed the previous season.

Andrew Brace, who had been brought through to elite level by Dave McHugh, did travel as an assistant referee, but it was just a little early for him to be selected for the main job.

So it was the first time that Ireland did not have a ref in both the Six Nations and the World Cup, not a good moment. Reflecting on events, it seems that things began slipping after those tournaments.

Following McHugh's abrupt dismissal, the slippage was complete by the time Japan came around. It's hard not to believe that his retention might well have changed that picture.

Despite their lack of World Cup recognition, honourable mentions must also go to Gordon Black, Bertie Smith and Leo Mayne, who all made enormous contributions to the elite game at European level and deservedly won their 'caps'. Even if it was a brief stay at the summit, they still had climbed the mountain.

Chapter Twenty-Two

3 November 2018

England v South Africa at Twickenham
(Autumn international)

The match was in the dying seconds at 12–11 to England when Owen Farrell cut down Springbok centre André Esterhuizen, with Farrell's shoulder heavily involved. A penalty would have given the visitors a chance to sneak a win but nothing was given. The referee Angus Gardner and his TMO decided all was fair and the match ended in an England win.

That, and many other tackles, were of a variety that was clearly dangerous in my view, and the officiating around it was completely inconsistent. The Six Nations and European Cup matches that followed the next spring saw more of the same, and that, added to the violent clearouts at the breakdown, saw my anger and frustration growing.

In that mood, I picked up the phone and called Gerry Thornley, rugby correspondent at The Irish Times, *with whom I always had a good relationship. I used the phrase that 'rugby was becoming a licence to assault'. He suggested I write down how I was feeling and he'd give it to his boss; it appeared in the paper a week later.*

With the 2019 Rugby World Cup on the horizon, I met with Thornley and his boss, sports editor Malachy Logan. Taking a leap of faith, Logan signed me up for the tournament, and my career as a columnist began.

• • •

The media never, ever bothered me. I have always thought that they have a job to do and, by and large, they do it well.

Some referees suffer from high levels of media-sensitivity, and cannot wait to buy the papers as soon they come off the presses; they detest being criticised, but that comes with the territory. The *Sunday Times'* Stephen Jones was correctly critical of a referee on one particular occasion, who then took great umbrage with the journalist's words, telling me, 'Have you seen what that so-and-so has written about me? He knows damn all anyway.' I told him that the criticism was absolutely justified and to take it on the chin, and, anyway, hadn't he been jumping for joy when Jones had praised him some months earlier? I'm afraid we cannot have things both ways, as much as we would like. The old adage of 'other people's opinion of me is none of my business' doesn't really hold water when that opinion is right.

If I performed below par, then I'd expect some flack and, depending on the style of the journalist, it would be delivered in a variety of ways. Polite, measured comments such as *Irish Times'* Edmund Van Esbeck's *Owen Doyle will need to have much better days than today* would hit home far, far harder than the *Telegraph's* John Reason's *The referee was awful, as usual.* The latter being no more than meaningless copy-filler and subjective opinion, rudely expressed. Unprofessional.

In Paris during the 1988 Five Nations 'Le Crunch' game, England full-back Jon Webb bent down and stopped the ball with the palm of one hand and, in doing so, he stepped past the ball, then turned around to pick it up. It certainly didn't look like a knock-on but it was, and France scored from the scrum that followed. Equally, I could, and maybe should, have ignored it; in those days, that was an unspoken option. Nowadays, a mere fingertip will be whistled.

Reason decided that I was fair game for this apparently calamitous error and absolutely harangued me for it. Again, he was quite entitled to express his opinion. Towards the end of the season, he was in Dublin for Ireland's final fixture, and was seated at the press table for the post-match dinner. As I walked by, on the way to my table, he asked me if I thought he'd been too hard on me. 'Certainly not, Mr Reason, anything that annoys you that much is worth doing.' He was none too pleased, but it was clear that some of his peers approved of my comment. That remark was not exactly game, set and match; but at least I felt it was a decent return of service.

On another occasion, he did go a step too far. His comments on the performance of Stephen Hilditch in the bronze final of the 1991 World Cup bordered on libellous. Hilditch, although very reluctant to take a legal case, did the game significant service by so doing. He was not, for one second, looking for a penny for himself, but rather for an admission that the article was not acceptable and that it had questioned his integrity. The wording of the apology was agreed out of court and appeared prominently some weeks later alongside Reason's usual column.

When I took up my role in the IRFU, I invited all of the rugby journalists to Lansdowne Road. We met in the old Wanderers pavilion and, using a flip chart, I outlined what the referees were supposed to do – so no point in criticising them on these issues. On another chart, the opposite was outlined and these were the things that were fair game. I also joked that, of course, we'd prefer that their words were constructive and would not imply that the referee's parents had met once, but only briefly. I gave them my phone number and told them to call me anytime, any query. The only proviso being that they would not quote me without first telling me that I was on the record.

The Ref's Call

One journalist broke that agreement, and I never answered a call from him again, despite several apologies being left in the message box. The French call it *confiance*, we call it trust; without it, most is lost.

Following Munster's defeat in the 2001 Heineken Cup semi-final to Stade Français, caused largely by an incorrect decision on touch-in-goal by assistant referee Englishman Steve Lander, Van Esbeck called me. We spoke for some time, and he asked if he could quote me, I said yes, and he read out my words as he had written them down, to be certain that the quotation was accurate. That is professionalism of the highest order.

France v Scotland in the 1989 Five Nations had been a very entertaining affair, as it often is, and I had enjoyed it immensely. My habit was always not to be available to referee the weekend after an international, especially when the match was in Paris, where there were wine business people to meet. It was coming up to dinner time on the Tuesday after the match when I found myself in Montparnasse, La Rotonde brasserie, waiting for friends to join me. Leafing through the newspapers, *The Sunday Times* was quite glowing about the referee performance, while *The Telegraph*, of course, balanced that out, and then some. *The Observer* did not mention me at all, my name was to be found only below the teams at the end of the article, and that's probably the best place for it. All in all, though, I was feeling pleased about things, life was good.

Across the room sat a very pretty lady with her equally

handsome man. She was looking my way, and becoming quite animated as she chatted to her partner. Well, I thought, she must have been at the match. Her companion shrugged, stood up and approached me, bringing a restaurant menu with him. Would I sign this for his friend, Nicole? You bet I would. I smiled at her, and wrote a nice message before signing my name. The man read the message, looked at me, then dropped the now unwanted menu back on the table. 'But we thought you were that American actor George Peppard.' If only I had known their thoughts, I'd have been more than happy to oblige. But isn't life funny; even if your feet are only thinking of leaving the ground, you are brought back to earth's reality pretty swiftly.

I don't know what the figure is, but since the game became professional, the number of rugby print column inches has grown and continues to grow exponentially. And the consumer is well served in Ireland, a variety of opinions is presented in well-written pieces of journalism. With no bias at all, my rugby paper of choice is *The Irish Times*, led by their excellent and prolific chief rugby writer Gerry Thornley.

After finishing in the IRFU, I had taken myself back to France in spring 2018, only returning to Ireland to attend that year's autumn internationals. I had missed the day-to-day involvement in the sport since my retirement but with no plans to step back in, my own entry to the media end of things came about much by chance. Watching the impacts players were being increasingly subjected to, I had become so angry that I phoned Thornley to vent my spleen, and my first column followed shortly on that very issue. The 2019 World Cup in Japan was approaching, and following a coffee with Thornley and his boss, sports editor Malachy Logan, it was agreed that I'd write two columns each week during the competition.

Many people thought I was in Japan, but the writing was all done in France, working from the television. But the column seemed to appeal, offering a different slant on the game, and it has also proved a terrific way of staying in touch with the whole thing.

Ireland's stated aim was to reach the semi-finals, otherwise the campaign would be considered a failure. That message was conveyed by the performance director David Nucifora, even prior to that year's Six Nations.

From a refereeing perspective, it was already a failure, with no Irish ref selected to travel: a first.

The land of the rising sun, and its people, gave us all a fantastic tournament, but it also gave us Typhoon Hagibis, which placed the very existence of the tournament under threat as it unleashed its worst. The night before Scotland's crucial match with Japan, Hagibis wreaked destruction and two confirmed deaths, a toll that would tragically rise to 98 in the following weeks.

In terms of the weather, things were calm the next day, enabling the match to go ahead. Japan, a tier-two rugby international nation, were meticulously prepared by a top-flight coaching team led by former All Blacks Jamie Joseph and Tony Brown, and were not in the slightest bit overawed by the possibility of reaching the quarter-finals. They chucked the ball around, with support play and accuracy the order of the day. Before Scotland managed to get into the match, they had left themselves with a mountain to climb, falling 28–7 behind. It finished 28–27 and Scotland were on the way home.

The pool itself was hardly a group of death; Ireland and Scotland, both tier-one teams, had to face off against Japan, Samoa and Russia. Ireland got off to a really good start, with a bonus point win against Scotland, 27–3, but that was as good as it got.

The match against the hosts was a very strange affair, Ireland led 12–3 after 20 minutes, but contrived not to score again, with Japan racking up 16 unanswered points to win 19–12. The Irish visibly faded, and everyone watching, either in the crowd or on TV, could feel the inevitable approaching.

Joe Schmidt had controversially opted for Jean Kleyn over Devin Toner in the squad selection, and as we watched Ireland lose a couple of vital lineouts it was clear that Toner's prowess in that area was sorely missed. Nor were Ireland at all happy with the performance of Australian referee Angus Gardner, the Japanese being allowed to drive well past the ball at the breakdown, making it very difficult for Ireland to contest possession and create turnovers. Although the referee hardly cost Ireland the match, he certainly didn't help.

The Ref's Call

While Welshman Josh Adams finished the tournament as top try scorer with seven, Japan's Kotaro Matsushima and Kenki Fukuoka had nine between them.

The second-place finish in their pool saw Ireland face into a quarter-final against a New Zealand side who chose that match to put in their best performance of the tournament. Ireland, needing a best performance of their own, barely turned up. In truth, New Zealand were magnificent, but that didn't soften the pain as they crossed for seven tries, to head for a semi against England with an all too easy 46–14 victory.

When they got there, the All Blacks did meet a tournament-best performance, with England playing out of their proverbial skins. Having been pre-tournament favourites, the Kiwis were now odds-on to win the cup, but the English pack was all over them, Itoje, Lawes, Curry and Underhill rampant in a famous 19–7 English win.

Having ended the hosts' dream run in the quarters, before accounting for Wales in their semi, South Africa were waiting in the final, refereed by Jérôme Garcès, who became the first Frenchman to be honoured with that pinnacle of all appointments. He was kept busy, particularly at scrum time, as the Springbok tactic was to generate as many penalties as possible from that phase. It wasn't pretty as they went about their business, but their power manufactured five of them. Handre Pollard kicked 22 points and, with the Springboks rarely troubled, two late tries made it a final score of 32–12. Those tries are the only two South

Africa have scored in winning three World Cups – their their scrum dominance had yielded 15 points.

England had suffered the very early loss of Kyle Sinckler, but it's unlikely that he could have resisted the pressure from props Tendai 'The Beast' Mtawarira and Frans Malherbe. These two only played just over one half of the match and were then replaced by a fresh onslaughting pair, Steven Kitshoff and Vincent Koch. It was sheer brute force, brawn following more brawn, and a clear example of where the game of rugby was going.

The tournament will also forever be remembered for the plethora of red cards dished out. The tackle technique of leading high with the shoulder had been addressed prior to the event with the introduction of the 'high tackle framework', indented to guide referees to consistent decisions concerning foul play. All of the teams and coaches had been made aware that a clampdown was coming, but some did not seem to have prepared for it, nor was there agreement on what was or was not foul play, even though the framework was advised to them all.

It was somewhat shambolic, but the tournament would have been a terrible advertisement for the game if these tackles had been deemed to be lawful. The referees, now under the management of our own Alain Rolland, did very well to stick to their task. It was not easy.

But the abiding memory, for everyone, will be that of Springbok captain Siya Kolisi, born into the poverty of Port Elizabeth's township of Zwide, lifting the Webb Ellis Cup to the skies. In many ways it was meant to be, 24 years after Nelson Mandela had handed that same trophy to their then-captain, François Pienaar.

That tournament cemented my place as a regular columnist and I'm sure I've been helped by my inability to sit on the fence. I know that any piece written by anybody on any subject will not get universal approval, in fact it may divide opinion, but as long as it provokes debate and discussion, then it has served its purpose.

Brendan Fanning has been writing good stuff for a long time in the *Sunday Independent*, and former Ireland captain and Lion Donal Lenihan pens, and speaks, with all the authority one would expect of a man with such deep knowledge of rugby. I once shared a train journey with him, from Cardiff to London, and I knew a heck of a lot more about the game when we arrived at our destination than I had when we'd set off. Lenihan inscribed his autobiography to me, *To Doyler, I wasn't over the line for that Munster try at Ravenhill in 1989, but thanks for the points anyway*. It was of course an unintended pleasure to try and help Munster out, but memory says that they still only drew, despite my unfailing generosity. Lenihan's former team-mate and legendary out-half Tony Ward's *Irish Independent* column is also always worth a read.

Across the Irish Sea, the *Guardian*'s Robert Kitson is a top-class, knowledgeable rugby wordsmith, and never fails to get us all thinking. Stephen Jones too has never failed to provoke; he was ever present in my career, when I started and when I finished. His paper, *The Sunday Times*, also made a good move for Irish readers by adding Dubliner Peter O'Reilly to the mix.

But there is nothing like France's magnificent *Midi-Olympique*, a bi-weekly paper completely devoted to rugby union bar one page on rugby league. Page after page of opinions, interviews and match reports on everything from internationals and their Top 14 competition, to the lowest divisional rugby, it is an epic production.

Prior to one France v England match, I was interviewed in Paris; the final question was what I liked most about France. 'Well, the fact that you can stop in any small village, or at any roadside café, and be sure of getting great food was, and remains, high on my list. This compared very well to my neck of the woods,' I rambled on, 'where you'd be lucky to get a sandwich turning up at its edges.' This somehow turned into 'Francophile Owen Doyle Doesn't Like English Food'. Luckily, by the time that hit the streets everybody had flown home.

But has any writer ever put pen to paper with more beautiful and telling effect than Con Houlihan? Writing on Cheltenham, the late, great scribe memorably penned one of my favourite passages of his:

When Arkle stormed up the hill to his first Gold
Cup, few of his myriad admirers realised that nibs of
snow had started to come with the wind [...] And no
doubt there are decent men and women who will dip

into their imaginations at some distant date, and say that they were there – and they will be right.

And when, far too soon, all of Ireland lost the national treasure that was his fellow Kerryman Moss Keane, Houlihan quite beautifully wrote:

> I will remember him, too, in his favourite corner in
> in Cunniffe's pub in Currow and in Daly's next door,
> holding his own in the banter and sometimes doing
> more than that. He had toured the world but that
> little village on the Brown Flesk was his home and
> there his fame will last and grow as the brown
> waters run around the creamery.

Through the ages, sport in general has been blessed with wonderful commentators on both radio and television. The understated input of tennis' Dan Maskell was nothing less than a joy to listen to, or indeed sometimes not. When John McEnroe directed his vitriolic 'You must be joking' at the umpire, Maskell was silent; he let us watch, knowing anything he might add could only spoil the drama. When it all calmed down, it was something along the lines of, 'Oh dear, he won't want to watch that later on.'

Jim Sherwin, equally good at either rugby or tennis, also didn't talk to us too much. When one particular long and breathtaking rally was over, and the players seated for the change of ends, that's exactly what he said: 'Simply breathtaking.' And not another word.

Meanwhile, over on the radio, the commentators were as exhausted as the protagonists, gasping and calling for water, having had to word-picture every single shot for the listener. Maskell and Sherwin let the pictures do the talking, and no doubt had time to sip away on a refreshing Wimbledon Pimm's and reflect on their good fortune that they weren't paid by the number of words they uttered.

Michael Corcoran is absolutely brilliant on radio, one can all but see the play as he instinctively describes the rugby unfolding in front of him, his enthusiasm infectious. But if ever he went on to do television, there'd need to be a different approach. For television the 'less is more' dictum holds true.

There are many, many rugby television commentators out there now covering the myriad of professional tournaments and everybody has their favourite. None of them are likely to be too upset, though, if the clear winner is 'the voice of rugby' of yesteryear, Bill McLaren.

When we'd arrive at the ground before an international, we'd always ask who would be commentating, any of Nigel Starmer-Smith, Cliff Morgan or Bill McLaren would do nicely; but with not a hint of disrespect to the other two greats, the last named was my commentator of choice since childhood.

Walking the pitch an hour or so before kick-off, McLaren would seek us out, first rustling in his pocket to remove a tin of sweets; we would all be offered a famous Hawick Ball – hard, like butterscotch, but wonderfully minty. Then he would chat away, asking our latest news, what had we been up to, on and off the pitch, and some of this might be weaved into his meticulously prepared commentary.

And what of Morgan's description of that try for the ages when the Barbarians beat New Zealand in 1973. As Gareth Edwards regained his feet after his never-forgotten dive into the corner, Morgan uttered the poetic words, 'If the greatest writer of the written word had written that story, no one would have believed it.' He had but a moment to think that up, and we can but marvel at how he did.

Morgan was an excellent piano player and, like all Welshmen, he could really sing. During the 1991 World Cup, we were all travelling to Lille on a desperately wet night. He sat at the hotel's piano and welcomed each new arrival with a cheering rendition of their national anthem. When Stephen Hilditch, from Belfast, and I arrived, I wondered what he would play, but Morgan knew exactly what, and he tinkled and sang a lovely version of 'Molly Malone'.

In terms of today's TV commentators there are so many now that it's impossible to go through them all. But I have to confess to a soft spot for Eddie Butler; he was, after all, the captain of Wales for my first international. Mark Robson is both knowledgeable and amusing; no doubt that very genial commentator, fellow Ulsterman Jim Neilly, gave him an approving nod.

And now there is also punditry – the word 'pundit' deriving from the Hindu Sanskrit word 'pandit', meaning 'knowledge owner'. Unsurprisingly, some have more knowledge than others.

The actual match commentary is now supported by half-time and full-time analysis of the events of the day. Former players and coaches give us the benefit of their views and opinions, and, in general, these are instructive and inform debate. However, on occasion they can be ill-informed, and it's frustrating to hear an incorrect comment on rugby law being announced to the viewer, who may well take it as gospel.

In New Zealand, pundits can seem over-biased, and some of their otherwise interesting opinion gets to be questioned on that account. They have also been very vehement in criticising the red-card penalties for high, forceful and illegal hits to the head. While World Rugby was telling the referees what they had to do, former iconic All Blacks Christian Cullen and John Kirwan raged against these decisions. It undoubtedly made a hard job much harder. Of course, they are fully entitled to their opinion.

But generally, punditry is fascinating in a positive way, and is also very educational. Ronan O'Gara explains the intricacies of coaching, both attack and defence, in ways that are understandable to the layman. There's a lot more to his 'KBA' (keep the ball alive) philosophy than meets the eye. Lawrence Dallaglio and Brian O'Driscoll are an entertaining, informative duo. Former English international, now rugby writer and broadcaster, Ugo Monye is another who always delivers a balanced, well informed opinion.

These days there is also social media, and some of it is excellent. Many followers of rugby prove that they have a huge amount of knowledge, and post online opinions of high and interesting value. It gives the lie to the oft-stated view that rugby is too complicated, and impossible to understand. There is one hell of a lot of knowledge out there.

And then comes the downside, posts that are both abhorrent and cowardly at the same time. Words are written that are scarcely believable, with the authors hiding behind the anonymity of their made-up names. All that they really do is prove that racism, homophobia and bullying have never gone away. Anybody who reads them should feel nothing but disgust, but those targeted with these personalised attacks feel a lot worse than that, chilled to the bone.

Chapter Twenty-Three

9 March 2013

Ireland v France in Dublin
(Fourth round of that year's Six Nations)

*The scoreboard at the Aviva read 13–6 in Ireland's favour
but as France piled on the pressure at the five-metre line
with just under 10 minutes left, the green line was wobbling.
Quite literally in the case of Brian O'Driscoll, who had just
staggered out of a collision with 19-stone French prop
Vincent Debaty.*

*While everyone else in the ground roared as Rory Best and
Peter O'Mahony combined to force a turnover penalty, my
focus was on the Irish captain, who was clearly in no state to
continue.*

Yet, having been off the field as a blood substitution for five minutes, and with the scores now level after a converted Louis Picamoles try in his absence, there was O'Driscoll being waved back on after what seemed little more than a dose of smelling salts. Brave? Perhaps. Foolhardy? Undoubtedly.

As I left the ground at full-time, I was already wondering what direction the game was headed.

· · ·

As rugby union enters the early years of its second quarter of a century since abandoning the amateur ethos, it is still a very young professional sport. But it must surely reflect and wonder if it's all been worth it. Some of those eminent figures who, after the 1995 die was cast in Paris in favour of professionalism, opined that 'the game is gone' might well have been prophetic. It is utterly changed in the way it is coached, the way it is played and the way it is refereed.

In 2020, instead of celebrating the first 25 years of professionalism, World Rugby was on the receiving end of very serious news. The phrases 'early-onset dementia' and 'chronic traumatic encephalopathy (CTE)' loomed large, as a throng of former players put in notice of their intention to file a law suit, claiming that the governing body had not done enough to protect them. Now in their late thirties and early forties, these former players are suffering the appalling effects of these conditions; their future is grim.

The decision to allow pay for play has had other consequences too. Everything is now about the money and winning is the only reason for taking part, the old Corinthian spirit of 'taking part is as important as the result' has long since been flushed away. Performances and results: nothing else decides if a player gets a new contract or if the coach keeps or loses his job. And all of this in a sport which is complicated in its structure and where many referee decisions could equally go the other way. In short, rugby union is a sport that was never designed to be played for money.

As we have watched teams do everything to win, an original contact sport has become one of mighty legal, and illegal, collisions. We have watched tackling, previously around the torso or below, gradually rise up, until it has become necessary to introduce head-contact protocols to guide referees to the correct decision. Many of these so-called tackles are sickening and head injury assessments (HIAs), which really should be called brain injury assessments, have become commonplace.

Over the years, we have all watched some of these collisions with horror. And too often, more horror has followed when players, obviously concussed, have come back on to continue playing. When Ireland drew with France at the Aviva in the 2013 Six Nations there was no doubt that Brian O'Driscoll had taken quite some bashing. When he was taken off to be checked out it really seemed as if he didn't know where he was and very few were thinking other than that his race was run. But it wasn't, and he returned within a matter of minutes, when it seemed absolutely clear and sensible to look after him off the pitch.

And nearly 10 years later, it is still happening – in the 2022 Six Nations Wales prop forward Tomas Francis returned to the pitch against England when minutes earlier he had been seen to be completely unsteady on his feet, leaning against the goalpost for support. The Six Nations investigated the matter, and came to the obvious conclusion that Francis should have been immediately, and permanently removed rather than be the subject of a head injury assessment.

Even more recently, on Ireland's 2022 summer tour to New Zealand, prop Jeremy Loughman was astonishingly returned to the fray against the Maori All Blacks after a heavy blow to the head had clearly staggered him. Both sorry episodes are further black marks in the book of player welfare.

The entire way in which World Rugby has treated concussion has been criticised heavily by many former players and by expert medics. Their questions, over and above attempts to reduce head contact in training and matches, are around the HIA process and whether it's reasonable to take players off to be tested when there is a suspected concussion. When that's the case, the arguments to remove permanently 'on suspicion' are strong. So, too, with the return to play protocols that enable concussed players to be picked again a week later. It's impossible to find any scientific data to support or justify these protocols.

One of the most astonishing seven-day returns was that of Luke Cowan-Dickie, who was selected to play for the Lions in their opening match of their South African tour in 2021. Just a week earlier, he had been sprawled motionless on the Twickenham turf, having mistimed his attempted low-flying tackle playing for Exeter in the Premiership final. Sure, we were told that he passed the protocols, but it only served to reiterate the question of whether or not those protocols were fit for purpose. As recently as July 2022, they were altered to extend the period before a player who has failed a HIA can return to play from seven to 12 days, but what impact those changes will have, or what loopholes may be found, only time will tell.

And it's all being going on for a long time; in 2012 World Rugby decided to introduce a five-minute pitchside concussion assessment and to utilise it in the Junior World Cup that year.

This was done against the very firm, crystal-clear opinion of former Ireland full-back Dr Barry O'Driscoll, World Rugby's long-serving medical advisor and cousin of Brian. Under no circumstances would he accept it, seeing it as nothing more than a dangerous experiment on adolescents. Having resigned, O'Driscoll has continued to speak authoritatively on the question, even publicly expressing a preference that his cousin retire after another concussion later in 2013, this time against New Zealand.

It's very hard to understand why nobody has been listening. Those in high places really needed to pay a lot more attention to him and to others who share his views.

The problem facing neurology brain medics is that they are working in a very uncertain science. A player presenting with symptoms, after a heavy knock or a series of sub-concussive incidents, may undergo an MRI brain scan. But, at present, these are very unlikely to show any relevant damage and will not demonstrate brain deterioration or indicate functional disturbance. Neither can a forecast be made as to the future likelihood of dementia or chronic traumatic encephalopathy; that can only be ascertained by biopsy at autopsy. The post-mortem examination of former NFL players who passed away in their 40s has shocked neuropathologists, so great has been the extent of degenerative brain disease that they found.

But science is moving quickly now, and in the not-too-distant future, perhaps three to five years, technology will show much more detail in the living brain. Then any player, from school to professional, will be able to see the condition of their brain, and it will also allow the medics to be much more certain of what is going on. When that is feasible, it will be literally a game-changer. While this will be positive for the players involved, and allow them to make fully informed decisions as to whether to continue or not, it will not serve as an encouragement for the sport overall. It may, in fact, do the opposite.

Other forms of very dangerous tackling have also

developed. We now have the double-tackle, with one player going low and hard, another going high to prevent the pass; there are actually online videos that teach this as a 'skill', but when it's performed at high pace and velocity by two huge men, it can hardly be termed 'safe'. The no-arms tackle, where the so-called tackler goes low and at high speed into the shins of the ball carrier, leading with his shoulder but with no attempt to grasp, is another method laced with danger.

In all of this, the massive weight of players is also of huge concern. Regularly, men of 125 kgs to 140 kgs are tackling much lighter opponents, even legal tackles see heads whip-lashing violently. Boxing would not allow a lightweight into a ring with a heavyweight. The simple solution is to get players to de-bulk to attain a more equitable weight, and maybe it should not be dismissed out of hand – a maximum weight for each position.

Sure, players still have handshakes when the match is over, but during it have very scant regard for the safety of their opponents or indeed themselves. It is win at all costs. The legally established duty of care is but a long-forgotten memo. And the cost is proving very high indeed.

The names of great former players Steve Thompson, Alix Popham, Carl Hayman and more recently Ryan Jones – all terribly affected by early-onset dementia and probable CTE – are familiar to us, but now for all the wrong reasons. They would have been mere teenagers when the game went professional, and they grew up to fulfil their dream of playing for their countries. They were not looking at a sport that held any dangers of brain damage, back then it was not even a consideration. Thompson, whose truly wondrous long lineout throw-in the 2003 World Cup final started the move for Jonny Wilkinson's winning drop kick, remembers nothing of that match. Speaking courageously and openly on his struggles, he has become a very public face on the issue and has decided to eventually leave his brain to medical science. It is all too sad and too terrible for words.

Young players too, in their mid-20s, are retiring having suffered far too many concussions, and Lord alone knows what the future holds for them. It is inevitable that some will follow the tortuous path of the many who are currently suing World Rugby.

There is very little doubt that coaching expertise has had its own damaging effect on the game, and that is a very peculiar irony. Collectively, they have, literally and figuratively, brought the scrum – one of the great characteristics of the game – to its knees. The carry-on at scrum time amounts to what can only be called a form of cheating. World Rugby must take some of the blame here as they have shown little inclination to insist on what is written in the laws of the game, such as a straight throw-in.

It is in defence, however, where specialist coaches, often bringing rugby-league influences, have done the most damage – training players to close down space, and to prevent opponents passing by tackling high and hitting ferociously – they have done their job too well. The mode of play has inexorably become one of violent collisions, whereas in its previous existence it was a contact and evasion sport.

I am not sure that there is any enthusiasm to learn from history, but serious lessons need to be taken from what is currently happening. World Rugby has a highly qualified, high-performance committee, consisting of many of the leading international coaches. This committee has a major influence on how the game is played but it is surely a highly conflicted group, and thus unlikely to vote for radical change. An international coach who favours using the scrum as a penalty-generator is not going to quickly agree to the scrum law being refereed according to the book, and that's where the conflict of interest inevitably arises.

There are other player-welfare issues that are not being properly addressed. The number of replacements allowed is farcical. Eight players, more than half the team, can be changed, and often that is a split of six forwards and only two backs. These replacements are now key to winning matches and the arrival of the so-called 'bomb squads' or 'finishers' has an over-bearing influence on the outcome. It's palpably unsafe to have huge, fresh players charging at a fatiguing opposition. And, conversely, these 'bomb squads', and the players they replace, do not suffer from the fatigue they would do if they were required to play the whole of the match. If they had to last the full 80 minutes, it's likely that their physical weight and bulk would need to reduce, and that could bring benefits of its own.

The Ref's Call

In times gone by, there were no replacements, even in the event of injury. The rules were then amended so that substitutes could be used when a starting player could not continue, and that was generally adhered to, with no cheating. But next there was cheating, with players feigning injury or being so instructed.

It all got terribly complicated and, eventually, we arrived at the situation we have today. And it needs to be fixed. There has even been talk of 'rolling' replacements, with the coach being allowed to take players on and off up to a maximum number of changes. That can work in the amateur game to encourage participation, to give more people game time, but would be a disaster at the professional end of the things; and it would be another curse for the commentators. The temporary replacement law protocols are complicated, and can come into play for HIAs and blood.

Blood replacement and cheating combined to give us the Harlequins 'Bloodgate' incident in 2009. It was one of the darkest days in the history of both rugby and a great club, who were then coached by the former England and Lions number eight, Dean Richards. Leinster had come to town for the Heineken Cup quarter-final and, following a series of injuries, Richards was anxious to get his replaced out-half Nick Evans back on the pitch, as Evans' own replacement, Chris Malone, had been forced off injured.

To engineer Evans' return, wing three-quarter Tom Williams was led off with a blood injury. All seemed in order but it was not, far from it. It turned out that a fake blood capsule had been used. Worse was the emerging fact that the club doctor had utilised a small scalpel to cut Williams' gum, to allay the growing suspicions about the capsule.

The fallout was cataclysmic. Richards resigned, but did not avoid a three-year worldwide ban. The physio who administered the 'blood' got two years and a doctor came perilously close to losing her licence.

Richards, humbly I am sure, served his time and returned to coaching at Newcastle Falcons in 2012. He was one of the most affable of men during his playing days, both on and off the pitch, and that's how I, and many, will remember him.

And who will want to referee the game, the way things are going? It is approaching mission impossible. The pressure now is in multiples of what it used to be, and the onslaughts on social media are appalling. I started off reffing to stay in the game and to enjoy it. Who can actually enjoy it these days?

Maybe, when the match is over and all has gone well, there is still the old-fashioned sense of enjoyment and achievement, but there are endless meetings and reviews, to plan and prepare for each match, and referees in the modern game are required to carry out in-depth analyses of their own performances. And, of course, to respond to the criticism of team coaches – there is a very robust system to allow coaches to confidentially do so. It is non-stop.

Bit by bit, rugby refereeing has moved to a precision style

of officiating; it is now a fully scientific approach where few misdemeanours are ignored. In the past, we saw the great referees turn a blind eye to offences that had no effect on play, it was 50 per cent art and then the science kicked in for things which could not be ignored. It is a great pity.

Some time ago, a group of former Irish international referees met for an enjoyable and interesting chat. By way of a straw poll, I asked how many would do it now, and there were no takers. While every referee is a product of their own era and adjusts to the needs of that particular period, the current demands mean that today's referees need to be full-time.

Ireland's golden generation of referees benefited from having people of high calibre who were not full-time, but who held separate, often high-level, roles outside of the game. They would not have abandoned their careers to take up a full-time whistle, and they would have been right. At present, some of the full-time referees have been able to park their professional careers and, of course, they can perhaps fit in some part-time work. They are the fortunate ones; the full-time requirement, I am certain, excludes some who would otherwise be very useful indeed.

The brain-injury issue is the biggest challenge facing the game, and it is an existential challenge. If rugby cannot alter how it has developed over the past 25 years, then its existence, as we know it, will be in grave danger. We only have to look across the pond to the United States to see where it all might go. There, football's NFL has become a sport watched by millions but played by just a handful. It too has seen massive problems with brain injury and early-onset dementia, and the staggering amount of $1 billion has so far been agreed and provided, to make settlements to the players affected.

If rugby does not get its act together and solve this issue, then the next 10 years may well see a huge decline in numbers, and the sport could be facing a future that mirrors the NFL. It will be played in schools (and probably only elite streams), colleges and professionally, but the amateur club game as we know it will be at high risk. It may also be that some unions suffer more than others – what if a school player of today is diagnosed in five or 10 years' time with dementia? While it doesn't bear thinking about, parents are already asking serious questions.

I don't believe that is an exaggeration – and remember, there have been fatalities. In Ireland, we will never forget the tragic loss of 14-year-old schoolboy Benjamin Robinson from brain injuries suffered while playing for his school Carrickfergus Grammar against Dalriada in January 2011. But I am not so certain that we have learned from it. Our near neighbours France saw the deaths of several young professional-club academy players in recent years, due to injuries sustained on the rugby field.

World Rugby is not blind to the problems facing the amateur game, and recognises that it is under survival pressure and that the retention of players is at the core of the problem, participation is the aim. So they have introduced a raft of potentially usable different laws that may now be adopted by any union at that level. Basically, a list of 10 options are on the menu, including no scrum resets, team numbers can vary, rolling subs can be used and teams may agree that lineouts are not contested. It's impossible to say if this will have the desired effect on participation or if what will be a very hybrid model will hold the necessary appeal. It will take some years for any of that to become clear, but something was very definitely needed. It is a roll of the dice, albeit an essential one.

We have all listened to World Rugby's insistence that player welfare is the top priority on its agenda, yet it has been an open secret that there is a dispute over the correct-ness of many of the red cards given over the past few seasons. Particularly at the last Rugby World Cup, Japan 2019, which saw a mighty crackdown on high tackles. There are far too many influential people who regard some of these head hits as simply an unavoidable part of the game.

Throughout the past 25 years, elite coaches have been slow, indeed neglectful in my view, to accept that the safety of players must come first.

Take the challenge in the air and how that was dealt with at the time. It was left to the referees to sort it out, deliver the red-card sanction and then take criticism for their action. The example of then-Ulster full-back Jared Payne is pertinent. In 2014, he was dismissed in only the fourth minute of his team's Heineken Cup quarter-final loss to Saracens by referee Jérôme Garcès.

Saracen's Alex Goode was high in the air when the arriving Payne crashed into him, leaving the referee with no choice. But the furore around the decision was worrying. Many thought Payne had been very hard done by and that the contact was 'just rugby'. Goode was knocked out and stretchered off. Nevertheless, it took several seasons before it became accepted that this type of decision was the correct one in such circumstances.

Payne, very unfortunately, in 2018 became one of the many players who retired early due to the effects of head injury. Thankfully, and at last, we have seen a very significant drop-off in the number of similar challenges, where the arriving player has no real chance of getting the ball. But it took far too long.

The point to emphasise here is that until everybody, especially those at the top table, accepts that dangerous challenges must be the subject of the ultimate sanction, then the damage to the game will continue.

Over the past few seasons, the high 'tackle' has become one of the latest player actions to be debated. It is very sad that there is a discussion over these, and when a player's shoulders make hard contact with an opponent's head, there still seems to be disagreement with the referee's decision.

The so-called clearing out of players in the ruck is yet another debate, even, again, when very clear shoulder to head has been the hard point of contact. The argument that the player had no other option would actually be a joke if it wasn't so serious. Once again, the referee cohort is the one trying to clean up the game, but without the much-needed support of the coaches.

World Rugby talk about their protocols and their education and, yes, they are working hard on it, but what we have seen on the pitch since RWC 2019 does not reflect what they are telling us.

In 2021, the governing body brought in a so-called regulatory guideline to limit full-on contact in training to 15 minutes in each week. It is not yet binding on teams, although it's hoped to get sign-up for Rugby World Cup 2023. But it's completely unsure who will measure the minutes or how compliance will be monitored.

It will all depend on the coaches buying into the process, agreeing to it and implementing it. That won't be easy.

There was an announcement by World Rugby in 2021 that also had the support of eminent experts. It is termed the brain-health initiative, intended to educate players and others around the issues of dementia. It underlines that there are, in fact, 12 modifiable factors that can influence the onset of dementia, and only one of these is from brain injuries sustained in rugby. Others listed include obesity, smoking, excessive drinking, lack of social contact, depression, pollution, hearing loss, diabetes and hypertension.

Yes, dementia is a most complex condition, and we can all readily accept that these are likely contributors for dementia as people get older. But trying to persuade that young, fit rugby players who have persistently been knocked about the head are likely to have also suffered from these factors is a very long shot indeed. Perhaps it will form part of World Rugby's lawsuit defence.

And I am far from alone in having these major concerns that threaten rugby. There is a group of former international players, styled 'Progressive Rugby', who are lobbying World Rugby for radical changes in the way the game is played. They must be listened to; they have been at the coalface as all of these issues have come into play and few are better qualified to point to specific changes that would probably assist a solution.

The final comment, a question in fact, on all of this, has to be: What will the teenage Thompsons, Pophams, Haymans of today, and so many more, and their parents, decide what's best for their future, for their lives? It might well not include rugby.

There is another issue lurking in the shadows, and that is the sale of a portion of the commercial interests of the Six Nations and other European competitions to investment company CVC Capital Partners, who now possess a significant slice of the game. Other major deals are being lined up around the world, as unions, desperate for cash, seek similar investors.

There is much to worry about in these investments, which are, of course, bringing much-needed funds to cash-strapped unions. It is completely unknown what influence these companies will wield on things like competition format, scheduling, season planning, TV rights . . .

the list is endless. One thing is certain: they will demand big bang for their buck, and their job will be to sweat the asset and maximise returns. They have not put in their coin for fun. And when they take it out again, which they will do, it is imperative that they leave the game in pristine condition. But it is all uncharted waters.

Following protracted negotiations, and initial strong opposition from the players' union, New Zealand Rugby is concluding a NZ$200 million deal with Silver Lake, another equity investment company. If players are playing for the 'lake' rather than the symbolic 'silver fern', there's bound to be a demand for more money. How much of the investment will filter down permanently to the amateur game is unknown.

That is the same situation with all unions, where the vast majority of the money is spent on the professional game, income that, of course, it generates. At the same time, the equally vast majority of players will never earn a brass farthing, so it seems very odd that amateur clubs get only the crumbs from the table while the pro game, consisting of only a few hundred players in Ireland, gets whatever it needs. It's a conflict of interest as unions try to service both ends of the stick, and also a dilemma that doesn't look likely to be resolved soon.

The changing position of many clubs is a very big partici-pation worry and has to be a major concern for the union. While some clubs continue to thrive, there is a worrying number that do not, struggling at best to put out two teams, whereas, in the past, it would have had six or seven. It is impossible to see how that situation can be halted and then reversed.

All major unions face the same issues, and they are all looking at little else apart from the income streams. The amateur game needs to have a very clear vision of where it wants to go and a healthy level of funding provided to deliver that vision. Otherwise, it's likely to continue to flounder and to deteriorate.

The bottom line, however, is safety. World Rugby are the custodians of the game, and they have watched as it has become more brutal and dangerous. There is a massive responsibility resting on those in the corridors of power to make it significantly safer, and to leave the game in better shape for the next generation. And they should be accountable if they do not.

The governing body has a highly competent performance committee in place that includes many of the game's top coaches. Each union, too, has people who are very qualified to make proposals that would assist in bringing in safety measures that would reduce the ferocious force of collisions.

The way the game is played needs to change, the decisions made over the next five, maybe 10 years will dictate whether or not it is sustainable outside of the professional side of the things.

As we all take out our crystal ball and look towards the future, nobody can see with any clarity what is coming down the track. It all looks very murky and uncertain – and that is a poor omen indeed.

One thing is certain, though: the sport cannot be allowed to continue on its current chosen, seemingly inexorable, path.

There is a tide in the affairs of men
Which, taken at the flood, leads on to fortune;
Omitted, all the voyage of their life
Is bound in shallows and in miseries.
On such a full sea are we now afloat,
And we must take the current when it serves,
Or lose our ventures.

William Shakespeare *Julius Caesar*

(Act IV, Scene 3)

Afterword

A Golden Age of Irish Refereeing

The golden age of Irish refereeing probably began its journey after RWC 1999 and continued to about season 2016–17.

It was a great period and, at the peak, World Rugby figures saw Ireland referee 21 per cent of all tier-one Tests in a five-year period up to 2013, frustratingly being pipped to top place in the world only by South Africa on 24 per cent. England were on 16 per cent and Wales – alias Nigel Owens – on 10 per cent. We also headed the Heineken Cup rankings, followed closely enough by England and France.

But let's not forget what went before, and what was, undoubtedly, an inspiration for me. Ireland had always punched above its weight in international refereeing. The first one I can remember was Ulsterman Ray Williams.

The Ref's Call

On 15 February 1964 in Cardiff, when All-Black prop-forward and captain Wilson Whineray dummy-passed the last Barbarian defender and touched down under the posts, he brought down the curtain on a 36-match tour: won 34, lost one, drawn one. The loss had come against Newport, and they drew 0–0 with Scotland.

Williams was the man in the middle for that Murrayfield international, as he was for two more of the five Tests that New Zealand played on that tour. Considering that he could not referee the Irish match, that was effectively three out of four for the quietly spoken Belfast man, a unique haul. And given that the system in those days was for the touring team to select the referee for the international Test matches, it was an extraordinary honour for Williams to be chosen so often.

Then there was Munster's Paddy D'Arcy, one of the best on the international stage. Tall, imposing and with natural pace to burn, he would glide seamlessly about the place, never far from the action. He also knew how to speak to players, and would be firmness itself whenever the occasion demanded; that really came as no surprise – as the county manager for Kerry, in real life, he had plenty of communicating to do.

Many, many years later, he was in St Vincent's Hospital for what would sadly prove to be his final weeks. I received a phone call from his son: 'Dad asked me to give you a shout, he'd love you to drop in.' It was both an honour and a tremendous pleasure. I saw him several times and found that nothing had really changed – a witty, knowledgeable, informative man. And a great referee.

Headmaster Kevin Kelleher certainly did not have the pace of D'Arcy, but he had an uncanny sense of anticipation, inevitably ending up in the correct place, even if he had walked there. In an era when international matches were far, far fewer than nowadays, he refereed 23 internationals, 22 of them in the Five Nations. Famed, of course, for sending off Colin Meads, there was a lot more to Kelleher than that single decision.

Willie John McBride's Lions in South Africa invented the '99' call and, at the end of that tour, it came back to Europe and to Ireland. It was a call that McBride felt was needed in order to prevent his players being physically intimidated. As if. So, if and when the punches came, it was '99' time and every Lion would join in – a case of 'one in, all in'. It also left the referee in a dilemma; he certainly couldn't send them all off, and it was impossible to pick out one player over any other.

Kelleher announced the solution: he would send off the last man to run in and join the fracas, on the basis that that player was the one with absolutely no excuse for getting involved in something that had nothing to do with him in the first place. It was good thinking: the last man would be judged to have the least excuse. As a young referee, I went to see this refereeing tactic in action, I think it was Fergus Slattery's Blackrock club who were playing. The

'99' call went out and everybody rushed in, then everybody suddenly stopped, looking around to make sure they weren't going to be the last man, so the call fizzled out. And wasn't seen again.

'Ham' Lambert of course was another, and had been the main influence in my starting off. But he did not just contribute on the pitch and, when he retired, he became, without knowing that it would later be so called, the first 'referee coach'. There are few who have reached the final destination of international rugby without having benefited from his brilliant and treasured advice.

Wales went to Twickenham in 1974 to play England, and Irishman John West was selected to referee his first international. England went offside at a scrum, penalty to Wales, but West had blown a fraction before an advantage developed, just as Phil Bennett was mesmerising the English defence with a trademark jinking side-step. Well, the referee wasn't the first, or the last, to be hoodwinked by Bennett's feet.

Later on, Wales considered that they had, at last, got the winning try; with J.J. Williams chasing a very long kick ahead, the ball was loose over the English line, and all of Wales saw him winning the race to the touchdown. Now, Williams could probably have murdered a 100-metre race in a little over 10 seconds, and that is not a requirement for any referee. West, with no TMO to sort it out, could do no more than call it as he saw it, and denied the flying winger a winning try. That moment went down in folk-lore and was probably the inspiration for troubadour Max Boyce's ballad 'I am an Entertainer' about 'blind Irish referees'.

Later on, West remarked that if he could have kept pace with Williams, then he wouldn't be refereeing but instead would be playing for Ireland. Probably right too. Nonetheless it was an inauspicious beginning to a very distinguished career, which also saw him break important ground in New Zealand when the French toured there in 1979. The southern hemisphere unions had previously been 'suspicious' of the quality of the referees from up north, but here was someone who they found very easy to accept. By then, the events of that First Test were but a distant memory – except, of course, in Wales.

In 2021, a Welsh supporter ran onto the pitch during their match against South Africa, nearly knocking over Liam Williams in the process. It has since been rumoured that this guy has pushed West down into second place on the list of the most unpopular men in Wales; if so, it's taken some time.

Wales went to Twickenham in 1980 to face archrivals England, and Dave Burnett of Dublin's Wanderers club was in charge for what was just his third Test. The match turned out to be bloodbath, no more, no less. Burnett later described it as 'the dirtiest match I ever reffed'. A total of over 30 penalties spoke volumes.

The Ref's Call

Paul Ringer, the Welsh flanker, had 'put himself about' the previous week in Paris and he started off in similar fashion against England. But he was not alone and the opening quarter was explosive. Burnett was absolutely clear in his message, which came after 13 minutes, the next player who offended would leave the pitch.

That necessary message, though, spoke to the inevitable – with only 13 minutes played, and given the awful atmosphere and bad feeling between the teams, it seemed clear that the match could not possibly finish with 30 players walking off together. And it didn't.

Following a lineout, the ball went from Steve Smith to out-half John Horton, who got his kick away. Ringer charged through on Horton and hit him late and hard on the head with his arm. That was that: he was rightly off.

In the dressing room after the match, England were counting the number of stitches inserted by the medics, and there were plenty in the Welsh dressing room too. But the numbers that counted for the most were the scores, and England won the match, 9–8.

Burnett had actually reffed me in school, having also started off at a young age because of an injury. While the Ringer dismissal should not define Burnett's splendid career, it is a subject that, similar to the J.J. Williams incident, is still remembered in Wales with a lot less than affection. Recently, its 40th anniversary was 'celebrated' – remember, the Welsh are nothing if not a passionate rugby nation.

Owen Doyle

As previously mentioned, Burnett, due to a twist of fate in the form of an unexpected French semi-final win, probably missed out on the 1987 World Cup final. At the conclusion of his active days, he continued in the role of international referee assessor and selector for the IRB, and made a great contribution to the IRFU referee committee.

My own club, Old Belvedere, was the location for a dinner in June 2005 to celebrate all of the previous international referees, and the new ones too; we had some party. The occasion was the presentation of actual rugby caps, which the IRFU had decided to award to all international referees, past and present.

That proposal had been delicately steered through the various committee stages necessary to reach fruition by John Callaghan, who was an excellent chair of the referee committee; we are all very grateful to him.

The old and the new mingled as if there was no age difference whatsoever, Alan Lewis spending most of the evening chatting with Ray Williams. The following day, Lewis phoned me, 'Great evening, thank you. And Ray Williams – what a man.' The event was compered by none other than George Hook, who did it as a good turn for us. He had really done his research, contributing to a great rugby evening. Hook had been Connacht coach when, according to his esteemed memory, I allowed a drop goal by Munster's Ralph Keyes, which he firmly believes went 'about five metres wide', that denied his team a famous victory. So it was really quite a favour.

The Ref's Call

Comedian Billy Connolly told us once that being a legend really requires nothing more than 'rumour plus time', so, on that basis, I might perhaps one day qualify. But all of those pioneering referees of the past are the true legends.

Most of my time at the top was in the company of two Belfast school headmasters, Stephen Hilditch and Brian Stirling, and both are currently heading towards that 'legendary' status. Again, their achievements were motivational, and inspired plenty of referees to think, *Why not me?*

Hilditch's curriculum vitae includes three World Cups, the first one in 1987, then also 1991 and 1995. The last of these saw him appointed to the England v New Zealand semi-final, which was the furthest any Irish referee had gone until Alain Rolland's final in 2007.

During the 1991 World Cup, Hilditch and I trained together and, in between his self-rolled cigarettes, he would put in slightly more effort than I, a non-smoker, was prepared to do. We would force ourselves to near exhaustion, far more output than we'd ever need in a match. I would stop when, eventually, I felt I might start to feel queasy, then I'd sit on the grass watching, in fascination, as Hilditch continued until he was close to the point of nausea. It wasn't particularly scientific or pretty to watch, but it meant we were very fit, maybe one more than the other.

Stirling's first international, England v Fiji, was in November 1989, a time when the islanders' tackling was even more ferocious than it is today. Body checks and high hits abounded and, as the match headed towards its conclusion, there were already two Fijians sitting in the stands, having been dismissed by the referee. And then another of those so-called tackles came in. Stirling saw it, but asked me, one of his assistants, to confirm the number of the player. When I did, he realised that he'd already given that player a warning, so, with not much time left, he quickly decided that 'a final, definitely final, warning' would be quite enough. He was spot-on.

When the golden age began, it came from having all the right fundamental development systems in place and the key objective of being determined to become the best. While the achievements of McHugh, Lewis, Rolland, Neville, *et al.* have been rightfully lauded in these pages, the example of those who had come before, in what was a fundamentally different amateur game, set the tone.

By the end of it, Irish referees had performed in innumerable Pro14 and European Cup matches, including six finals of the latter, the pinnacle of the club game in Europe. Not to mention a quite remarkable tally of over 250 international Test matches, which included, of course, the 2007 Rugby World Cup final. If anybody had told me at the outset that that would be the result, I'd have suggested they take a running jump or, more probably, have bitten their arm off.

For all those referees of this era, it was a time they will surely treasure for ever, they were on top of the world, and did themselves and the IRFU proud. None of it will be forgotten.

Acknowledgements

This page is really a series of very well meant, sincere thank-you notes, and that's just as it should be. There were many who suggested and then encouraged me to complete this project, below are just a few.

First, to all of the top-class team in Hachette Ireland where Ciara Doorley and Jim Binchy took the initial leap of faith that made it all possible, thanks to Joanna Smyth and Elaine Egan for their work on the book, and to Stephen Riordan for his help with the photo section.

Tony Considine came on board later and deserves enormous credit and thanks for his ability in putting order and structure into the book. We worked really well together and he always went that extra mile. I am very grateful.

Billy Stickland was a young photographer when I was starting out with the whistle. Through his sports photo agency, Inpho, he has been more than helpful in researching images that have been used in the book.

Owen Doyle

It's impossible, of course, to overlook Malachy Logan of *The Irish Times*. As sports editor, he gave me space to pen a column which was my first essay writing since I was at school, and that was not today or yesterday; another leap of faith.

Whenever I had occasional doubts, my two sons, Mark and Ian, were on hand to give much-needed treasured words of reassurance. It was always along the lines of 'go for it, there is no doubt.' Great stuff, really important.

A special word for the truest of all friends, Terry Hayden. He was always ready, more than able, and especially willing, to bring me to a pleasant watering hole and forget about writing for the evening. We studied wine lists instead.

Another rugbyman, fellow francophile Welshman, Ben Hughes, poured copious cups of coffee, and also interviewed me, in the most impeccable French, for his local La Rochelle radio station.

Lastly, but very much not leastly, my partner Terri. Also known as the Minister for Fun, her never-ending, smiling patience and tolerance are a far cry from my own. I was fed and watered at all the appropriate, and even inappropriate, times and given every inch of the quiet time I needed, and that was one heck of a lot. It's not possible to thank Terri enough.

Finally, I've tried to be as accurate as possible with dates and the order of events but, if some are not spot on, please forgive me.

Photograph Permissions

Owen Doyle